BURIED IN MAINE

A Tour of Maine Cemeteries and the Stories that Accompany Them

Arend T. Thibodeau

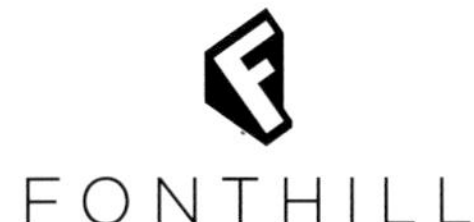

FONTHILL

Fonthill Media Inc.
www.fonthill.media
office@fonthillmedia.com

First published 2024
Copyright © Arend T. Thibodeau 2024

ISBN 978-1-62545-145-3

Typeset in 10pt on 13pt Sabon
Printed and bound in England

Tread lightly, she is near
Under the snow,
Speak gently, she can hear
The daisies grow.
All her bright golden hair
Tarnished with rust,
She that was young and fair
Fallen to dust.
Lily-like, white as snow,
She hardly knew
She was a woman, so
Sweetly she grew.
Coffin-board, heavy stone,
Lie on her breast,
I vex my heart alone
She is at rest.
Peace, Peace, she cannot hear
Lyre or sonnet,
All my life's buried here,
Heap earth upon it.

O. Wilde[1]

Preface

No matter what our station is when we come into this world, we are given but one assurance, and that assurance is that each life must end. Since time immemorial, humankind has tried to reason with this assurance in an effort to understand and come to terms with the concept of death.

In Australia, Aboriginal peoples believe that the planet Earth is a vibrant spiritual landscape that humans never lose their connection to. With the belief that we are one with the earth they practice a symbolic ritual of burying umbilical cords to signify the connection the Aboriginals have with the planet. In the Christian faith, a great golden kingdom called Heaven is the destination of the pious, and with this comes the belief that Heaven is not a place designed after the creation of our world, but rather, a parallel realm that originated along with the rest of creation. A place where the omnipresent God is surrounded by devout spirits in a community of peace, love, and worship. On the other end of the Christian spectrum, a place called Hell awaits those who live a life without God's influence and commit violations of God's laws. In Norse myth, Valhalla awaited those who died with honor; there, the fallen would feast on the meat of a magic boar in the great hall alongside the mighty Odin.

Whether you believe you will return to the earth, reside in paradise, an anti-paradise, or any of the other final destinations that make up our vast and differing human belief systems, the fact remains that we are all going to die. This book is an examination of that fact, and a look at the aftermath of our departure from this plane of existence.

This book will visit cemeteries that have hosted the departed since the early colonization of Maine. Angels of death, thoughtful epitaphs, and even intrigue surround these old and unique burial sites. I will visit graves such as the Jonathan Buck grave in Bucksport. Buck, a forefather for the town of Bucksport, allegedly had a curse placed upon him by a condemned witch as the book will explore. I will visit some other notorious gravesites in Maine and the resting places of famed authors, artists, and community leaders.

As a photographer, my journey through Maine cemeteries is a photo documentary, and I attempt to capture images that tell stories in and of themselves. There is an adage that states a picture is worth a thousand words and I try to consider that, allowing the pictures to "fill in the blanks," aiding in my textual depiction of these places and things.

Legends, hauntings, curses, scenic cemeteries, and unique gravesites are explored while examining philosophies of the afterlife and writings of intellectuals. In addition to facts, histories, and details, I will also offer personal experiences and poetry.

Edgar Allen Poe wrote: "The boundaries which divide life from death are at best shadowy and vague. Who shall say where the one ends, and where the other begins?"[1] As Poe suggests, the answer to the age-old question of where we go from here is ambiguous at best, and this book will strive to maintain that ambiguity.

Contents

Introduction

Ever since evolution enabled our brains to utilize abstract reasoning, logic, and philosophical concepts, we have been plagued with the same quandary. For more than 3,000 years since the advent of documentation, we see evidence of the same questions repeatedly. Questions that cannot be answered despite the millennia of trying as well as the leagues of academic brainpower dedicating considerable time (often a lifetime) to them. Why do we exist, is this all there is, and if not, where do we go from here? Despite our big brains we cannot solve this riddle, and we cannot understand why we have so much power of reasoning and logic only to have it taken away when our synaptic pathways cease to fire neurons; as the life fades from us, so must we too, fade into oblivion. Or must we?

The afterlife is a *Homo sapiens*-only club; its exclusivity is maintained by a complex set of rules or guidelines that must be followed and are established through myth. Placing coins on the eyes of the dead for passage on the river Styx, a semi-complex set of commandments handed to Moses to establish a social charter, the list goes on.

Written centuries before the bible, the Egyptian *Book of the Dead* indicates that the departed must be in possession of the book to allow them to navigate the afterlife; if they are not in possession of the book, the complex set of spells and magic contained therein would prove too difficult for the layman's mortal soul to discern and he (or she) would be devoured into nothingness. At the end of the day, it is this nothingness that we, as humans, are desperately trying to avoid.

In his 1952 poem "Do Not Go Gentle into that Good Night," Dylan Thomas suggested that we live a life of zeal and enthusiasm, and he recommends we rage against the nothingness created by the death of our light.

> *Do not go gentle into that good night,*
> *Old age should burn and rave at close of day;*
> *Rage, rage against the dying of the light.*[1]

Similarly, the Latin poet Horace suggests that no one is guaranteed any amount of time other than the moment in which they currently exist. "*Carpe diem quam minimum credula postero,*" translates to "sieze the day, put very little trust in tomorrow." His words were written in 23 BC, over 2,000 years ago, and they still ring true today with the message that life is fleeting, and each moment should be savored as if it were the last.

It is in the spirit of Thomas and Horace that I look upon these places of internment as celebrations of lives lived before me. I try to appreciate their contributions to the human record, no matter how significant they may be. Some lives may have been rich and full while others may have been cut short with pain and tragedy. To the point, I try to focus on the lives lived, and in some small way, I hope this book helps to contribute to the remembrance of those who might otherwise have been forgotten.

Death

I am peace and serenity
I am chaos and calamity
I am the fear in the room
and the calm in the corridor

I am always near
and can either be found
creeping in shadows
or glowing in the light

I'm the cold hand at your throat
I am life's final warm embrace
I am Death

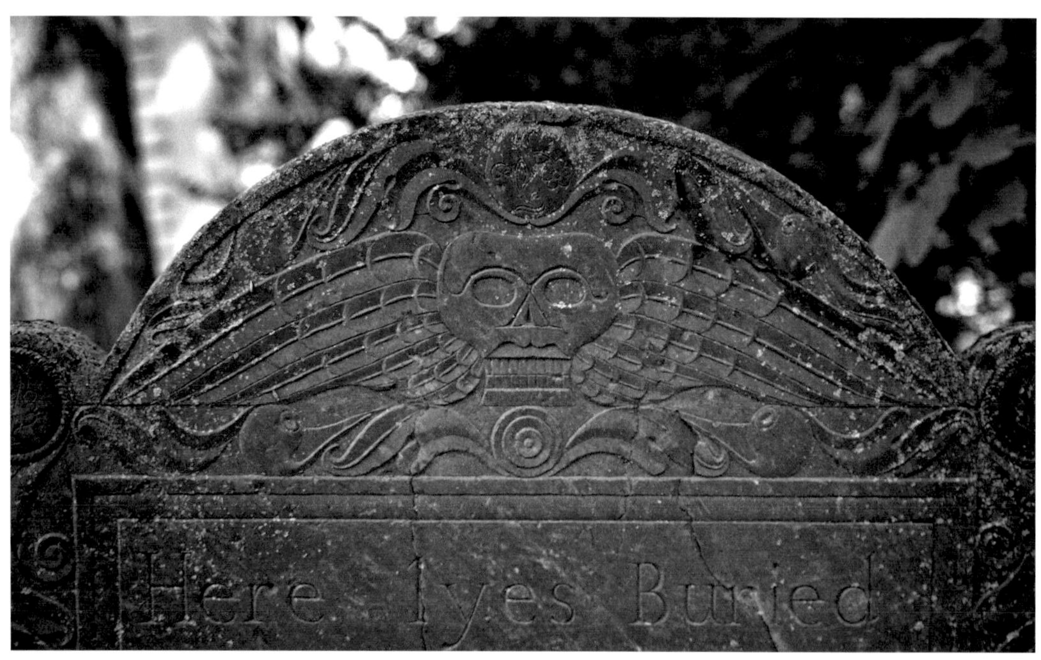

Detailed angel of death carving, York Burying Yard. Image used to accompany the poem "Death."

1

Early Settlement Burial Sites

Human beings have been inhabiting the area of Maine for thousands of years. Long before the Massachusetts colony and long before the European colonizers came to the shores of North America, many Native American tribes called the northeast their home. Yet even earlier in our human record, there is evidence of earlier tribes of humans living in the areas around Penobscot Bay and thriving on a type of swordfish that is now extirpated. These early humans are known as the Red Paint People due to the red clay they used in performing ceremonies and burial rituals. The Red Paint People were a maritime culture that lived and thrived in the northeast from Labrador to Lake Champlain; it is uncertain why they disappeared, but it is surmised that the fish they harvested became depleted and they simply moved on.

Large deposits of these people's red clay were discovered in the area of present-day Bucksport, and it is believed that there once was an established population of these early people along the Penobscot River.[1]

Maine's anthropologic history is rich, and its population timeline is vast. When we consider that the Red Paint People were here nearly 4,000 years ago, the seventeenth century does not seem that long ago.

Regardless, long after the Red Paint People, and long before it even became a state, Maine was colonized. It was mostly just southern, coastal communities at first. Ease of transportation by sea, along with resistance from inland native tribes kept the colonies close to water, and Pemaquid was one of Maine's earliest settlements.

2

The Pemaquid Burying Ground

I found the Pemaquid Burying Ground during a warm day in late May. The wildflowers were all coming into bloom and the first thing I noticed as I walked up to these colonial grave sites was how vibrant the wildflowers were surrounding the old slate stones standing in the field.

The burying ground is located close to the village of the same name and located within the town limits of Bristol on Maine's scenic coast. Pemaquid was settled between 1625 and 1628 and is one of the nation's oldest English settlements. However, Native Americans inhabited the area long before English settlers arrived and much of our knowledge of this era has been obtained through archeological discoveries.

The markers in this small seaside plot date back to the early 1700s, but it is suspected that this was a site for settlers to bury their dead since the area was first colonized in the 1600s. It is thought that many burials occurred beyond the boundary markers of the existing graveyard and there were accounts of mass burials after native attacks on the settlement during the seventeenth century. Early grave markers were simple stones or wood and did not hold up like grave markers that followed, so it is difficult to tell the expanse of the original burial areas. Record keeping during this time did not receive the attention it does in our contemporary society, and often the dead were also buried on private lots, as well as village burying grounds such as this one.

The existing markers on the grounds offer some good examples of colonial-era gravestones. The intricate etchings and angels of death that can be found on these early stones are good examples of the detail and efforts that went into hand carving these stones during the colonial period. Unfortunately, the quality of the stone that was used for the carvings on these graves was stone of inferior quality and the gravestones continue to deteriorate today, despite efforts to preserve them.

The carver for at least some of the old slate stones in the burying ground was Jonathon Sikes who was a member of a family of stone carvers in the area. He was known for using low-quality stone for his carvings, and there is record of him carving other stones in the surrounding areas.[1]

Against the background of the cemetery, the Pemaquid River offers a million-dollar view forever unseen by those interred in these grounds. As I explored the area, I was amazed to see some of the dates on these stones, all from the 1700s and very early 1800s. As I stood there admiring the view, I realized that many of the people buried in these plots were alive during the American Revolutionary War and the signing of the Declaration of Independence.

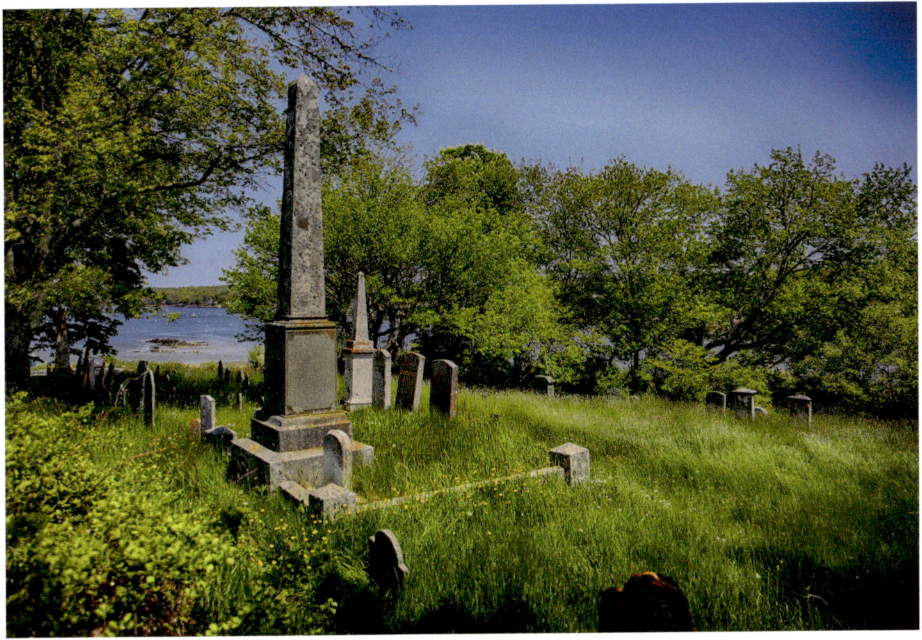

The Pemaquid Burying Ground is located near Fort William Henry. This image is looking out over the Pemaquid River and toward Pemaquid Harbor to the north.

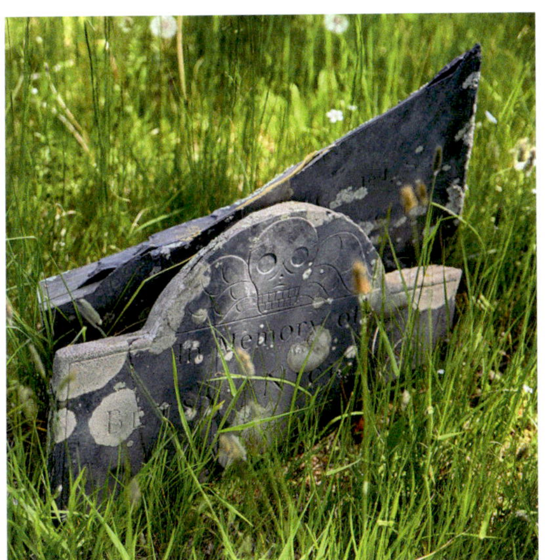

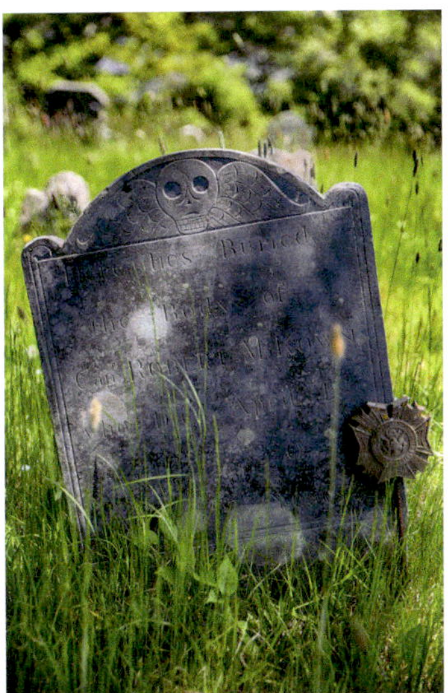

Above left: The abrasive salt air and harsh Maine winters no doubt contributes to the degradation of grave markers, but low-quality slate was also used and now the stones seem very delicate and brittle.

Above right: Captain Robert McKown died on April 1, 1776, just over three months before the ratification of the Declaration of Independence.

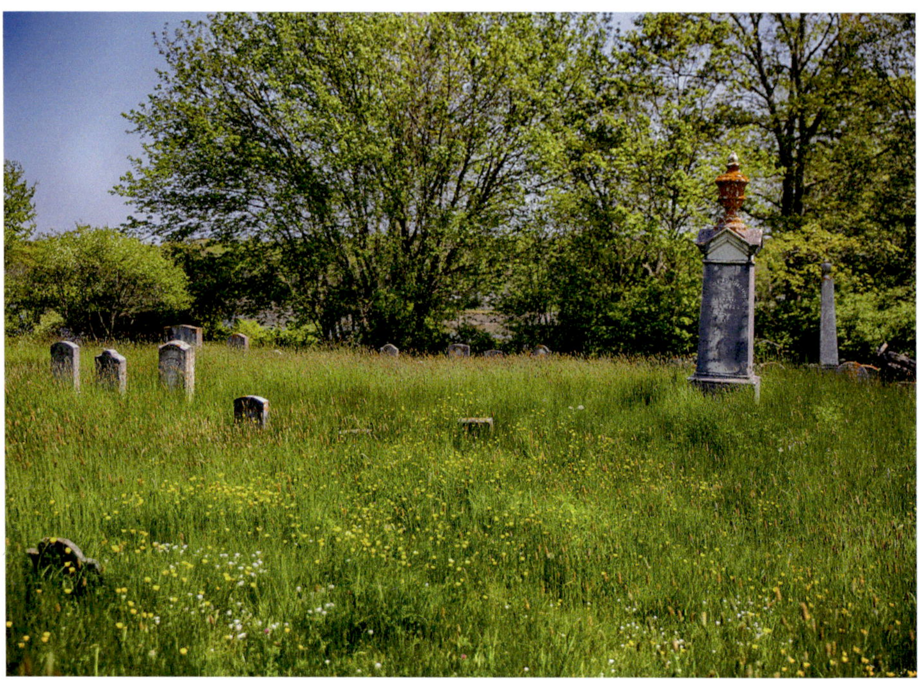

Wildflowers grow at the Pemaquid Burying Ground on a warm spring day. Image used to illustrate the poem "Wildflowers."

Wildflowers

The winds have blown their seasons
Time has come and we cannot reason

Just as a memory is a thing of the past
We are fools to think the moments last

So, before the sunshine turns to snow
Please visit me where the wildflowers grow

3

The York Burying Yard

The York Burying Yard is a slightly newer cemetery than Pemaquid. York received its first interment in 1705.

It should be noted, however, that the site is also the location of the 1692 Candlemas Massacre that occurred on January 24. The unprovoked attack on the village was carried out by Abenaki Warriors and resulted in an estimated fifty settlers being slain and close to another hundred being captured; many of which would have unlikely survived their treks through the wilderness back to the Abenaki tribe in late January.

So, it is uncertain how many people are actually buried in the area as accounts vary and recordkeeping at the time left much to be desired.

These are some of the best hand-carved slate gravestones I have encountered. Some of the angel of death etchings are meticulously done as is much of the lettering. The quality of the slate is also obviously high. Although I was only able to find limited information regarding the carver of stones in this area, when compared to both Pemaquid and the Warren settlements, it is obvious which communities were the most prosperous at the time and had the most resources.

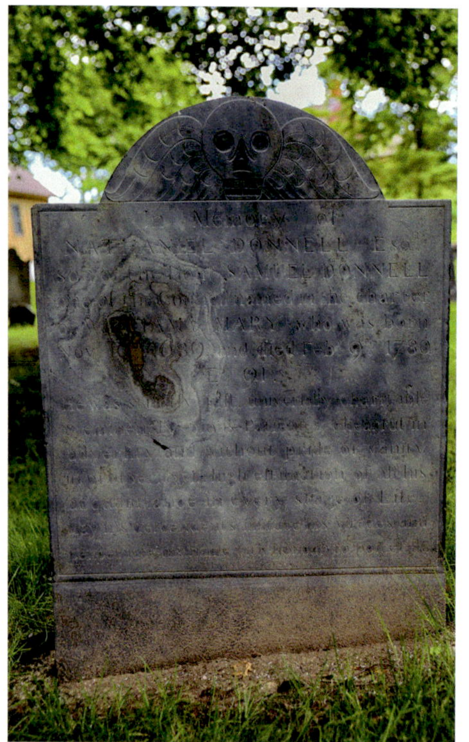

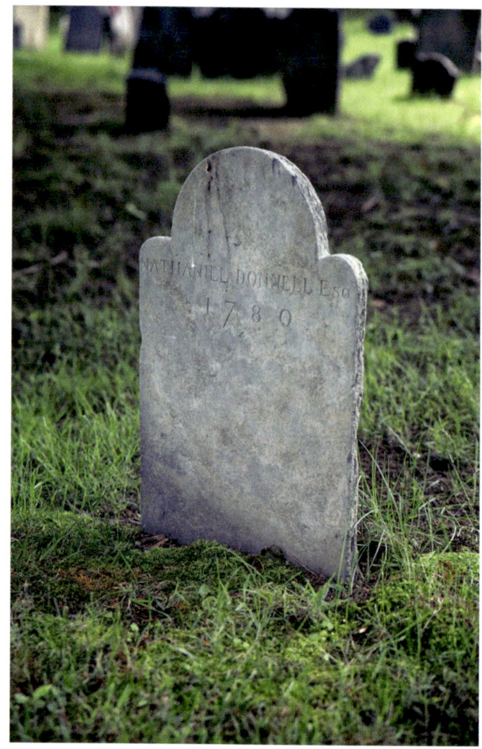

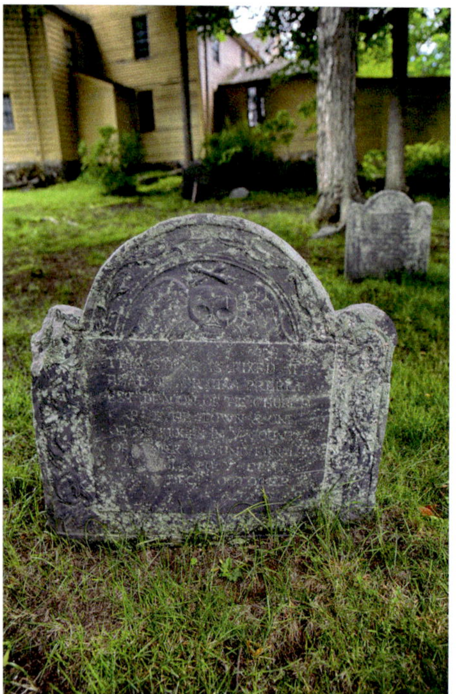

Above left: Nathaniel Donnell was a judge, justice of the peace, and one of the first councilors of Massachusetts. He died on February 9, 1780. The inscription on his headstone is a testament to his long standing in the community: "He was strictly just, universally charitable, and eminently pious, patient & cheerful in adversity and without pride & vanity in prosperity in high estimation of all his acquaintances in every stage of life. May his descendants imitate his virtues & perpetuate his name with honor to prosperity."

Above right: The footstone for Nathaniel Donnell. Footstones were often found in early burial areas but seemed to go out of favor. They are often just a smaller version of the headstone with nothing more than initials and a date on them.

Left: "This stone is fixed at the head of Abraham Preble Esq deacon of the church, Capt of the town & one of the judges in ye county of York; Was universally faithful to ye death/ Who died October ye 4th 1714."

Right: Jonathan Sayward was a self-made man; he was a wealthy merchant, shipowner, judge, and deacon of the church. Sayward was extraordinarily pious and committed to the values and beliefs of the church. A staunch conservative, he remained loyal to the crown despite his success in the new world, and he also professed a belief in witches when corresponding to John Adams. He died in 1797.

Below left: The growth on the stone of young Abigail Simpson gives it a unique appearance. Her stone is inscribed with, "Here lies the remains of Abigail Simpson who died Nov. ye 23rd 1715/ Aged 15 years."

Below right: John Bragdon was a young man who apparently strayed from the path of righteousness at some point in his life. According to his inscription, his soul was saved by repentance, but it was nearly too late. In the end, he died with "Some comfortable hope in his Death after great distress of soul & solemn warnings to young people, not to put off their repentance to a Death Bed." John's last day on earth was June 19, 1774. He was twenty-three years old.

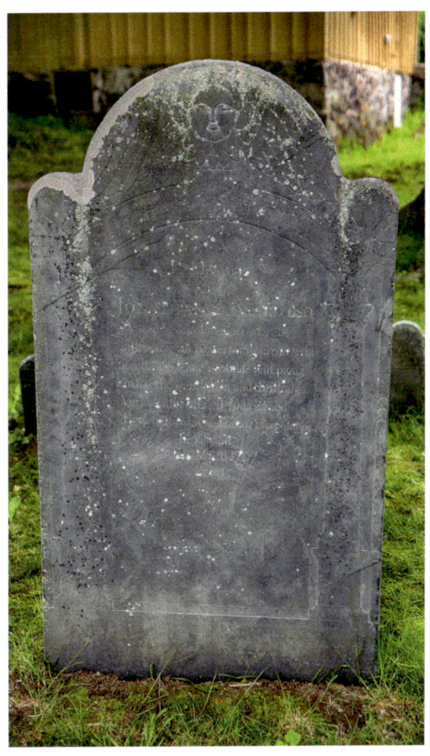

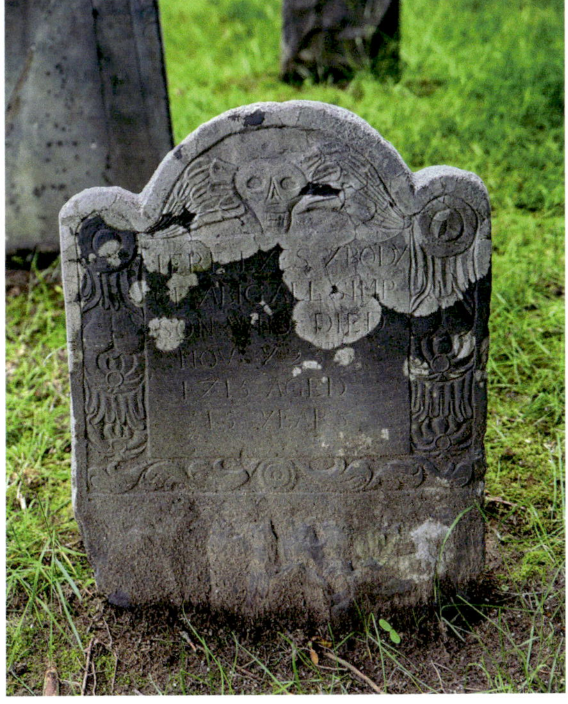

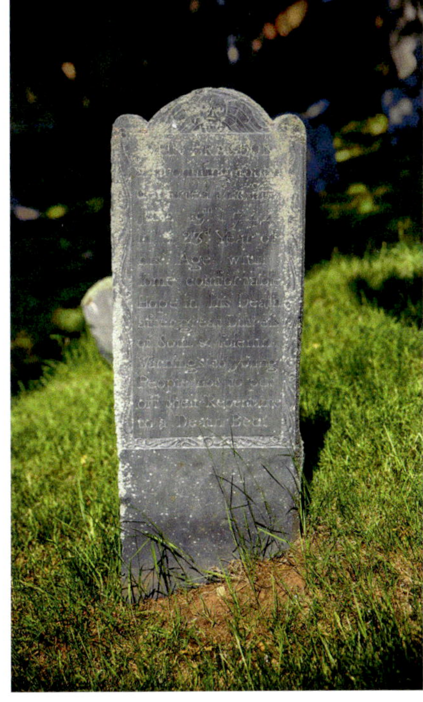

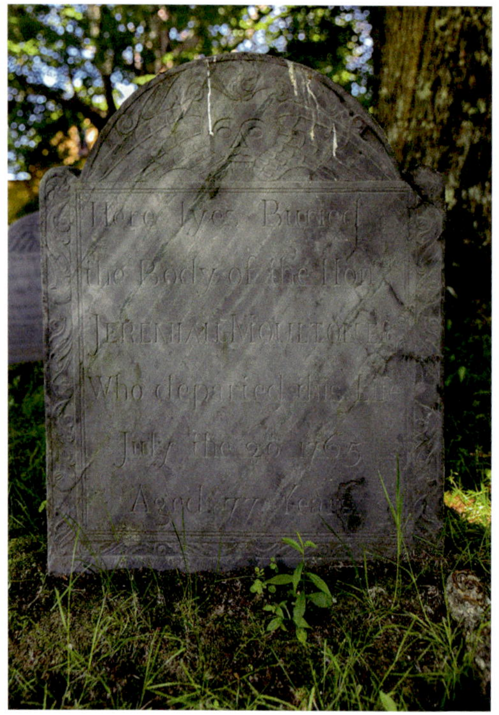

Jeremiah Moulton was a probate judge, father, husband, and militiaman. He is purported to have had the nickname "Indian Slayer" because of his reputation for treating Native Americans with fierce hatred after having been orphaned as a toddler during the 1692 Candlemas Massacre.[1]

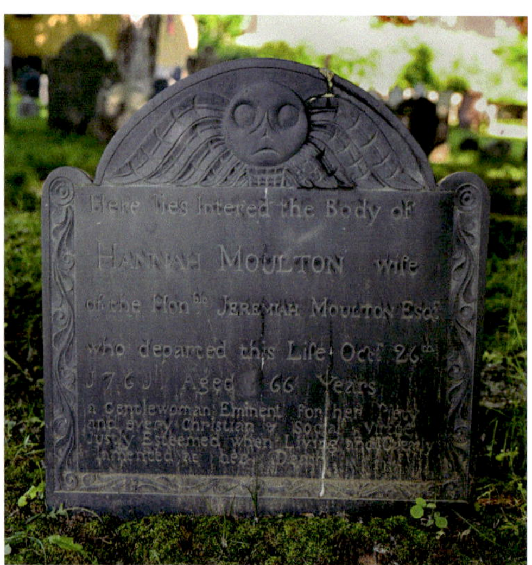

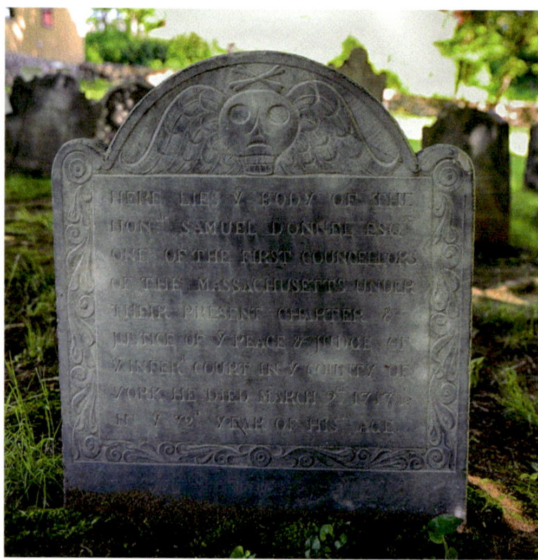

Above left: Hannah Moulton was the wife of the Honorable Jeremiah Moulton. By all accounts, Hannah was "A Gentle Woman eminent for piety & every Christian and social virtue, justly esteemed when living & greatly lamented at her death."

Above right: "Here lies ye body of the hon'r Samuel Donnell Esq'r. One of the first councellors of the Massachusetts Colony under their present charter & justice of ye peace & Judge of ye Infer'r Court in ye County of York who died March 9, 1717, in ye 79 year of age."

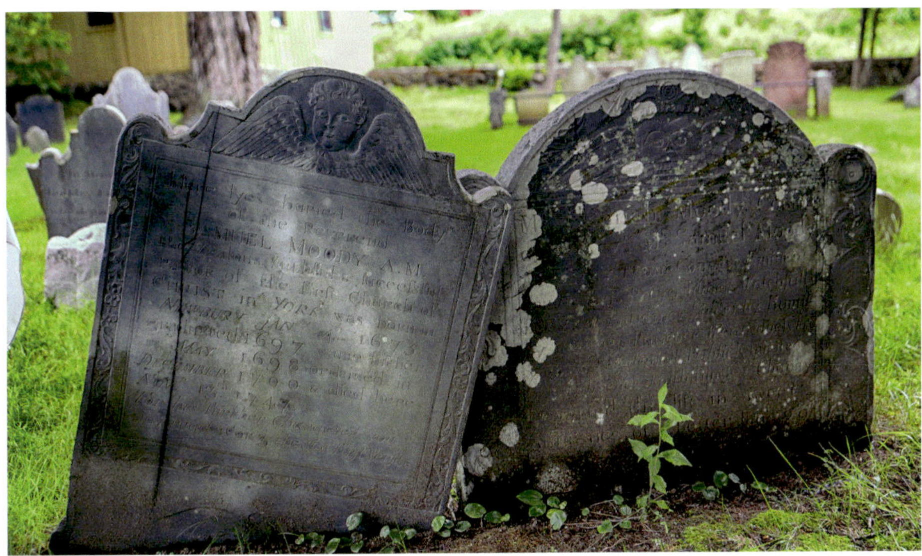

The stone of Reverend Samuel Moody (L) and his wife, Hannah (R). Samuel Moody was a devout and zealous preacher who had strict puritan values. His inscription reads, "Here lyes buried the body of the reverend Samuel Moody A.M./ The Zealous, faithful and successful pastor of the first Church of Christ in York was born in Newbury 1675, Graduated 1697, came hither in 1698, ordained in 1700 and died here Nov. 13, 1747."

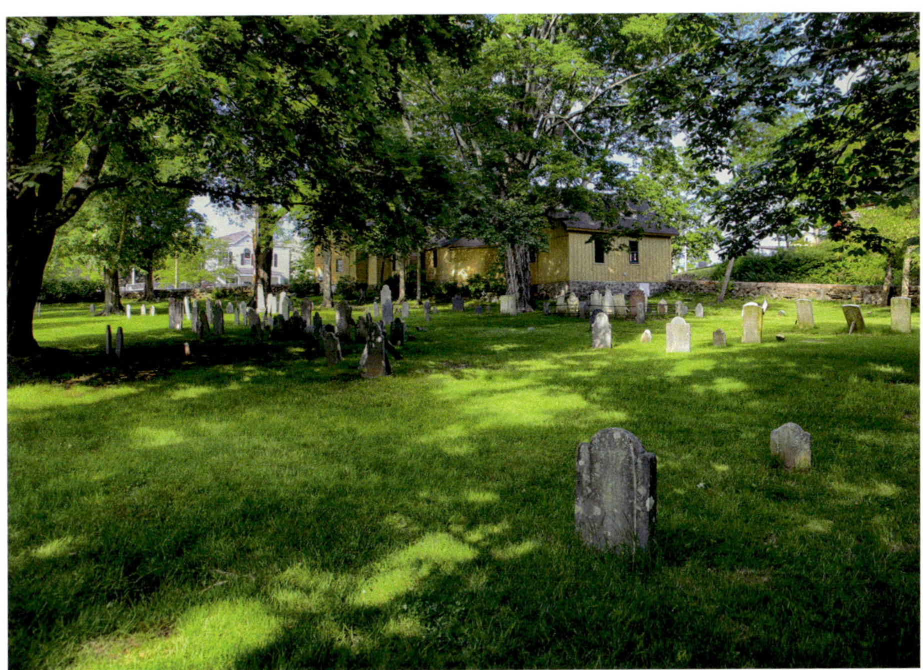

Although there are a few outlying gravesites, most of them are concentrated in this central area of the burying grounds.

4

The Settler's Cemetery

The Settler's Cemetery is located 3 miles outside of Warren along the St. George River. It is the most recent of my three choices of early settlement sites and it is the most derelict and out of the way. The site was used from around 1736 until sometime around 1792. Further, it is the only one of the three settlement yards I selected that is not in an area that developed into a community. The site once held a church and the settlers had plans to erect a meeting house which never seemed to come to be.

The Warren Historical society states that a church once stood at the site, but there was no indication as to when the church was removed. The site along the river is nearly a half a mile from Route 1 and visitors are not allowed to access the cemetery by automobile, making it a difficult cemetery to visit.

The graves are a potpourri of field stones, unmarked sites, and slate markers, which make it very difficult to see how many interments there are. A survey conducted in 1985 determined there are twenty-two graves on the property. The few slate markers that are present are very deteriorated and difficult to discern. I suspect that a lower quality of slate like that of nearby Pemaquid was used. It is also likely that the same family of stone carvers was employed.

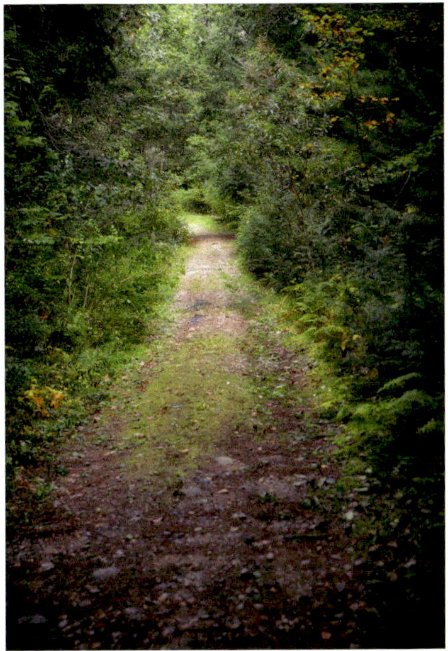

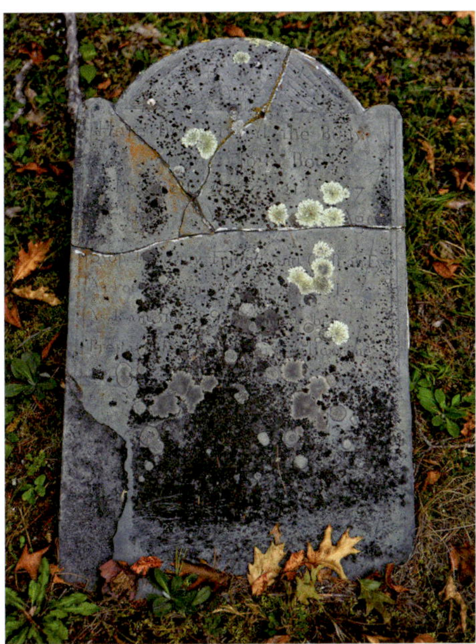

Above left: The cemetery is quite a distance from the developed areas of Warren. On the walk in, it is easy to consider what it might be like traveling on the unpaved, narrow roads of the past.

Above right: The grave markers are all in very poor condition; this stone was lying flat on the ground, broken and faded from the elements. I was able to discern that it is the grave of John Bogs who died December 21, 1773.

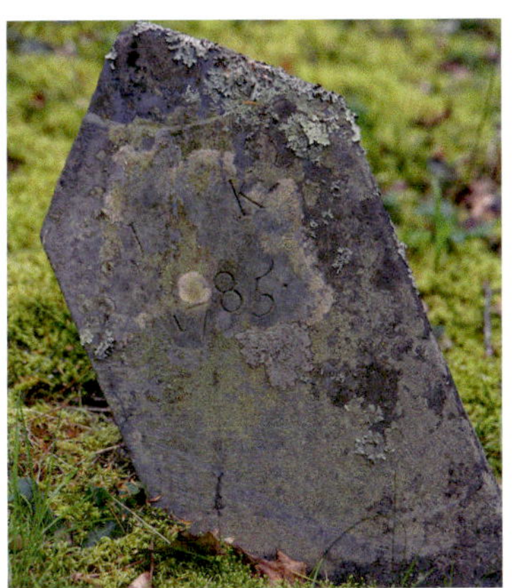

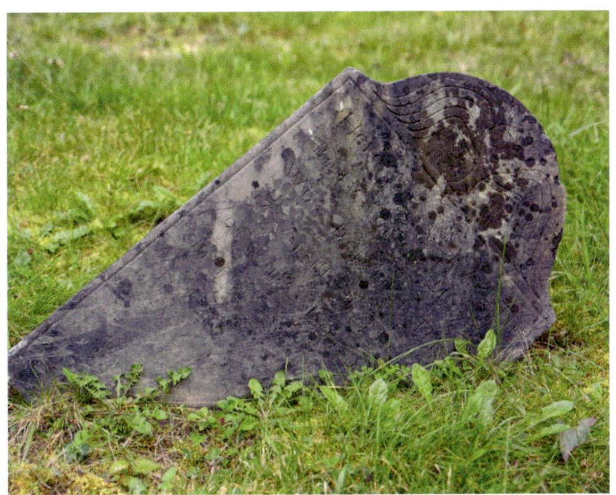

Above left: This marker was simply marked with the initials "L. K." and the date "1785." The stone is slowly sinking into the ground at a slant. It may have been a footstone at one time, but the headstone is not present.

Above right: Mary Shibles, April 17, 1771. The death's head that is carved on this stone is one of the most unique I have encountered.

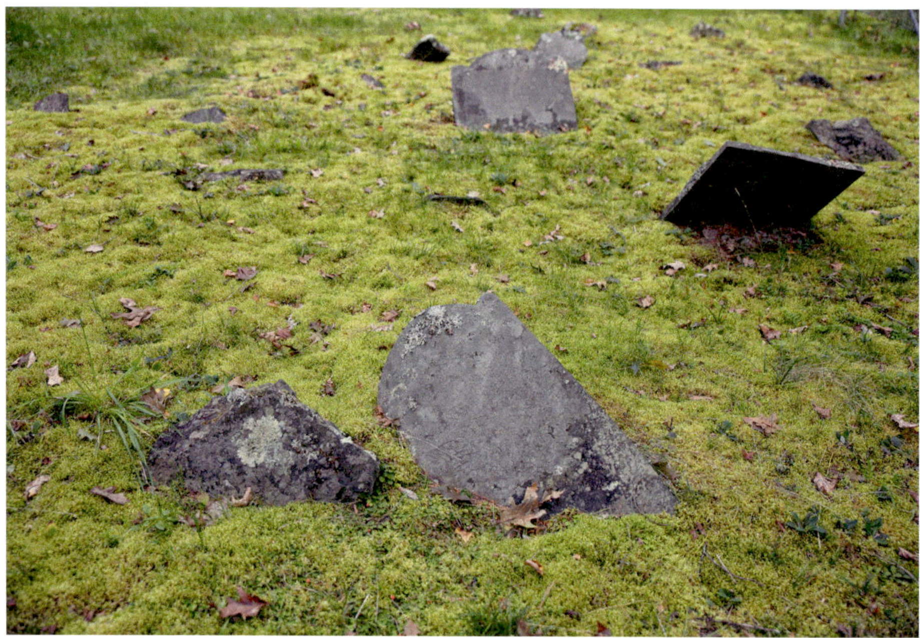

The gravestones are in an advanced state of degradation and are no longer upright. It is difficult to discern exactly how many are buried here, but according to a 1985 survey, there are twenty-two interments.

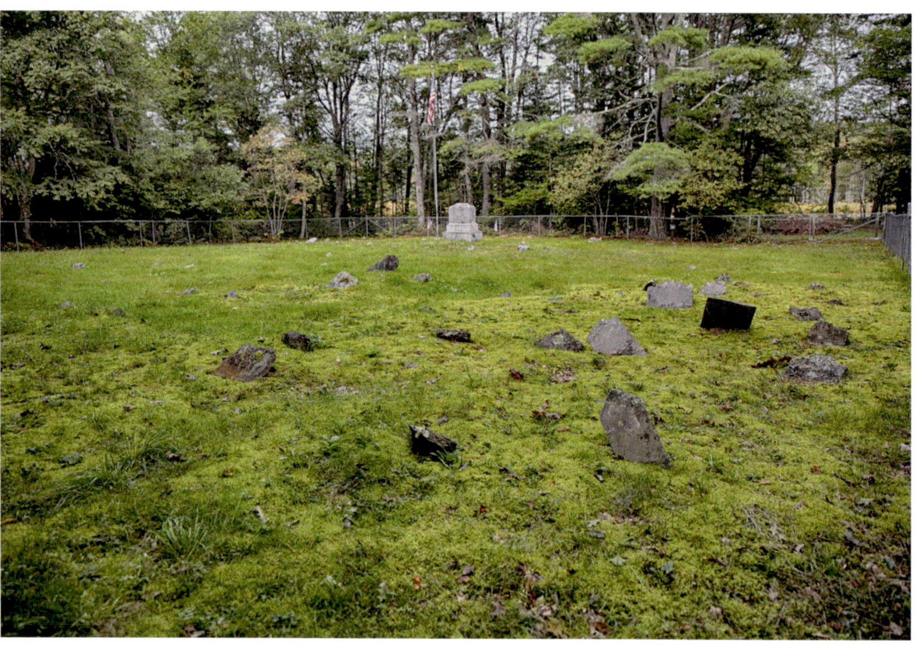

To protect the area and preserve the graves that are unmarked, or modestly marked, fencing was placed around the cemetery.

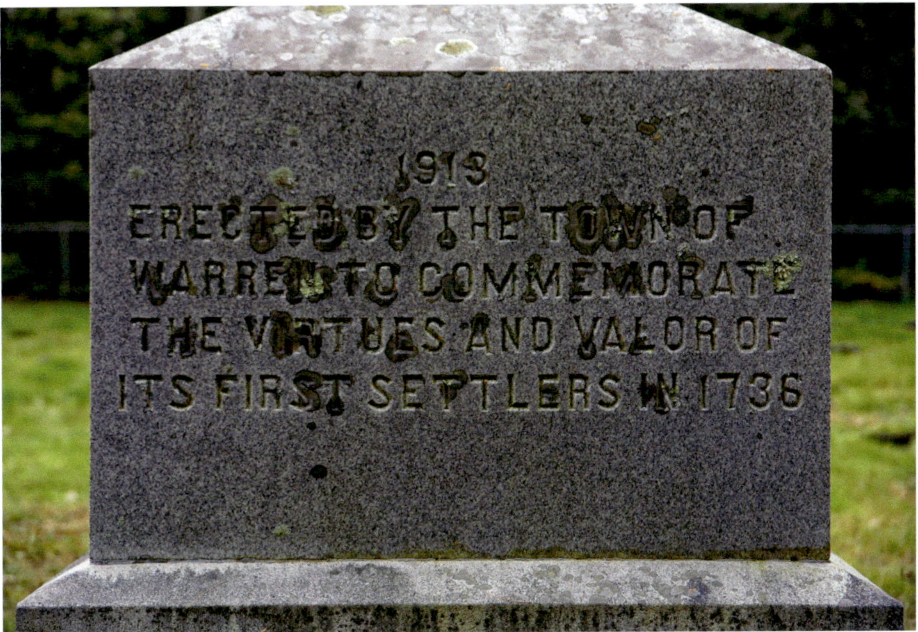

In 1913, residents of Warren placed this marker on the site to memorialize the settlers who paved the way for this Maine community and honor those who were buried without proper markers.

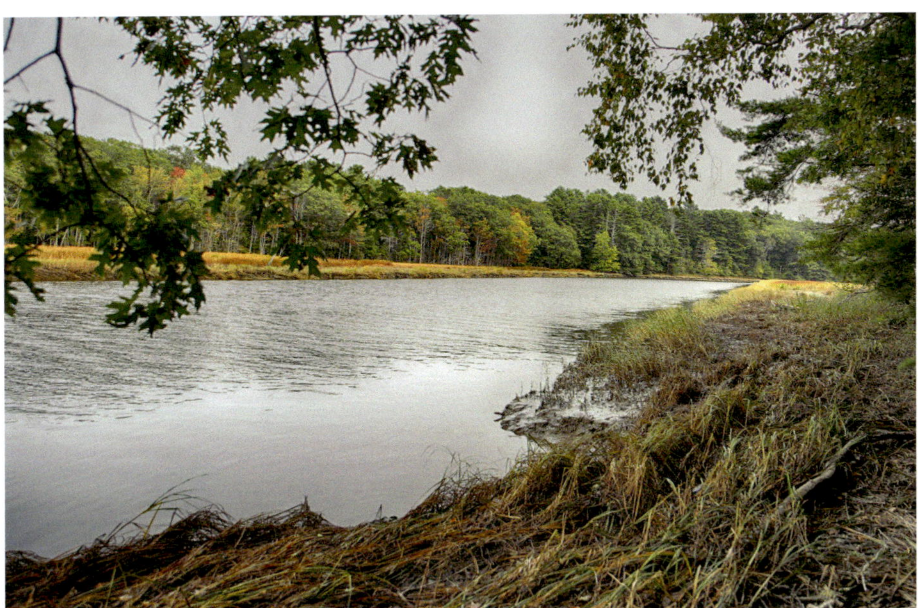

The area surrounding the cemetery is largely undeveloped and its location along the St. George River is serene and peaceful. Despite the out of the way location, traffic can still be heard as it robustly travels the busy highway less than a mile away.

5

Famous Graves

It was difficult to make selections for these next three sections. Maine has had so many talented artists, writers, musicians, and celebrities, it was not easy to decide what or whom to feature. I thought it logical to select a poet, an author, and a visual artist.

Edwin Arlington Robinson

Edwin Arlington Robinson was a life-long Maine resident and three-time Pulitzer Prize-winning poet. Robinson's career was not a clear one, nor was it easy. He was forced to return home from Harvard University in 1893 and his family's finances went into decline. He endured years of poverty, rejection, and obscurity until finally being recognized for his craft, winning not only the Pulitzer Prize for poetry in 1922, but in addition, it was the first year the Pulitzer committee awarded a prize in poetry. He went on to win the prize again in 1925 and 1928.

Robinson's poetry was reflective of his life experiences in that it was expressive of the difficulties and tragedies of life. He described his childhood as unhappy and he tragically lost both of his brothers, one to a drug overdose and the other died a pauper in a charity hospital.[1]

Robinson reasoned well with the topic of death; as an example, I selected stanza 3 of his poem "For A Dead Lady" from his 1910 collection *The Town Down the River*:

The beauty, shattered by the laws
That have creation in their keeping,
No longer trembles at applause,
Or over children sleeping:
And we who delve in beauty's lore
Know all that we have known before
Of what inexorable cause
Makes Time so viscous in his reaping.[1]

Robinson died of cancer in a New York hospital on April 6, 1935. He is interred in his hometown in Gardiner, Maine.

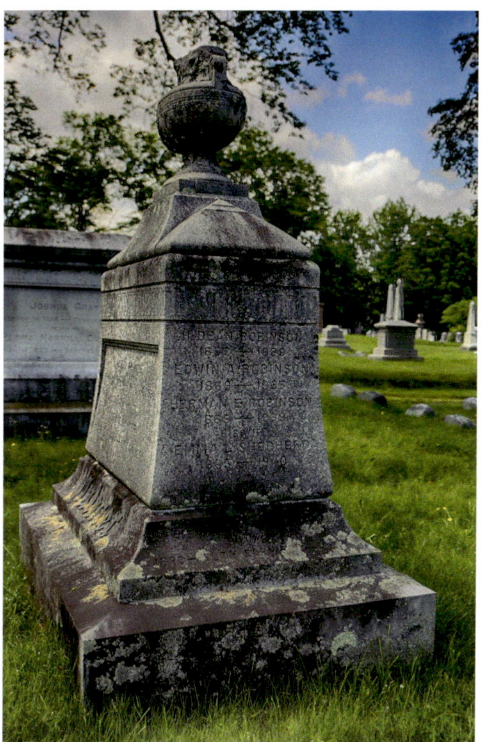

Robinson's memorial he shares with family
at the Oak Grove Cemetery in Gardiner.
Robinson lived a solitary life, never married,
and never had children.

E. B. White

Elwyn Brooks (E. B.) White was born in Mount Vernon, New York, in 1899. He enjoyed
a prolific career as a poet, essayist, and regular contributor to *The New Yorker*. White
would often visit his summer home, a farm in Brooklyn, Maine, with his wife. It was
on one such visit when he saw a spider in his barn and was inspired to write the classic
children's tale, *Charlotte's Web*.

Charlotte's Web is a profound story of morality, the cycle of life, and the necessity of
death. The book was an examination of life and friendships along with the trials and
tribulations that accompany both.

White's profound philosophy on accepting that which must come to pass is voiced
through the character of Charlotte, an artistic spider who saves a pig from the
slaughterhouse.

"You have been my friend," replied Charlotte. "That in itself is a tremendous thing. I
wove my webs for you because I liked you. After all, what's a life, anyway? We're born,
we live a little while, we die. A spider's life can't help being something of a mess, with
all this trapping and eating flies. By helping you, perhaps I was trying to lift up my life
a trifle. Heaven knows anyone's life can stand a little of that."[2]

White's everlasting message that we should leave things better than we found them
by striving to make the world a better place and helping others is one that continues to
resonate with children and adults alike.

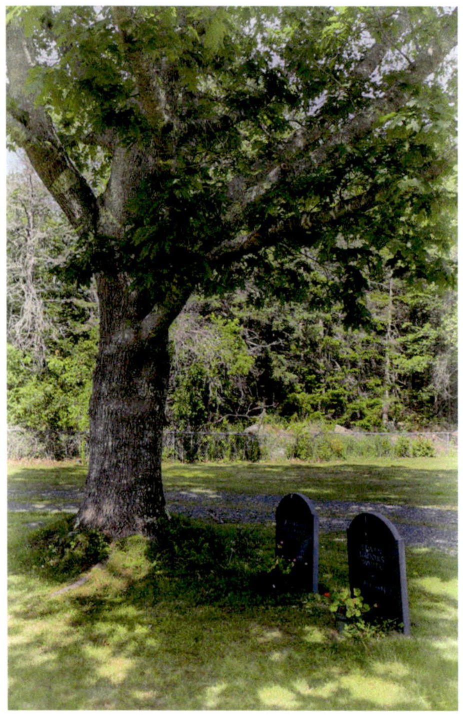

Left: The grave of E. B. White alongside his wife, Katherine, who died in 1977. White suffered from Alzheimer's late in his life and passed away in 1985 at age eighty-six.

Below: The small coastal community of Brooklin is where White is interred. The cemetery is in a quiet part of town and is an active cemetery.

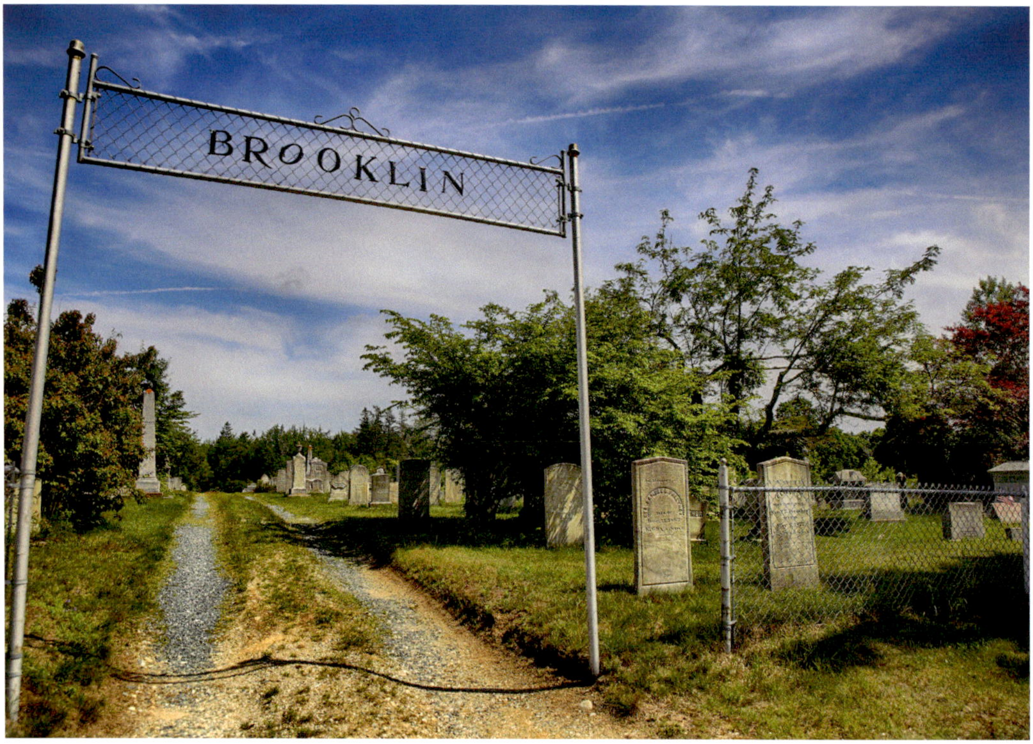

Andrew Wyeth

Andrew Wyeth was born in Chadds Ford, Pennsylvania, in 1917 where he grew up and trained to be a painter with his father. Wyeth sold out his first gallery show in 1937 and continued to gain acclaim with his attention to detail, mastery of lighting, and photographic realism.

Wyeth's best-known painting, *Christina's World* (1948), is a portrait study of Anna Christina Olson in the field near her home. Olsen suffered from polio and had difficulty getting around which Wyeth depicted with raw emotion and realism. The painting is considered a contemporary masterpiece and is currently in the possession of the Museum of Modern Art in New York.

The Olsen house is located near the grave site in Cushing and was the home to Anna Christina and her brother Alvaro Olsen who were close friends with Wyeth and his wife, Betsy; the Wyeth's would come to their summer home in Maine where Wyeth spent a great deal of time with the Olsen's at their home. The Olsen House is recognized as a National Historic Landmark and was the inspiration for more than 300 paintings and sketches by Wyeth.

Visiting the site is a surreal experience. Not only did I feel as though I were in the presence of greatness, but also interred here is the artist's muse, and the location of his most profound inspiration. I am unable to put it into any more elaborate words than that.

This location should be a pilgrimage destination for all artists.

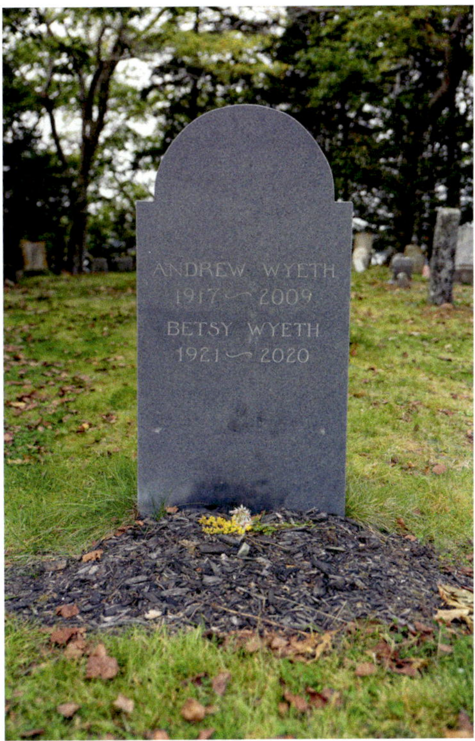

Andrew Wyeth's gravesite near the water's edge on Hawthorne Point Road in Cushing. He is interred with Betsy, his wife of sixty-nine years.

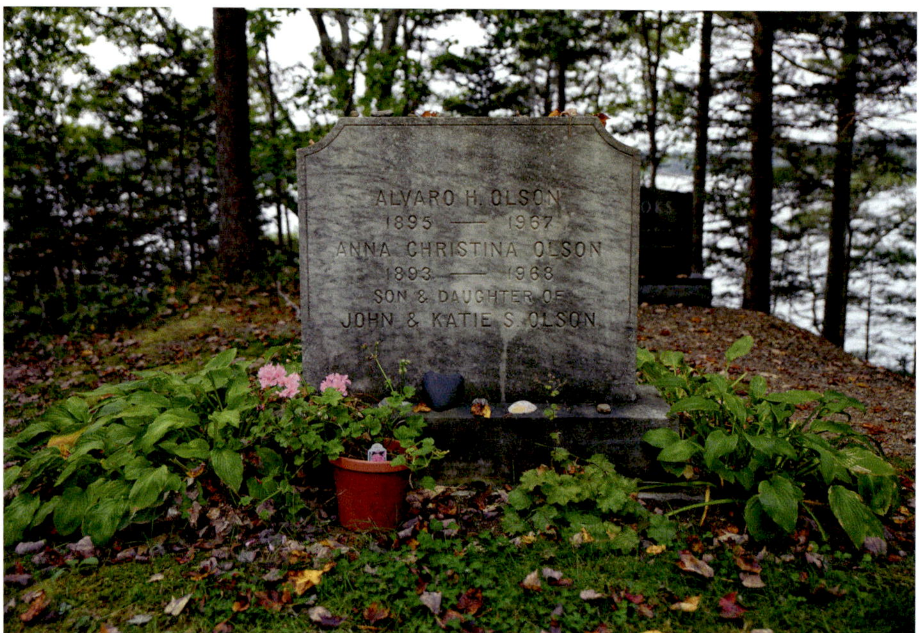

It was both awe inspiring and surreal to visit the grave of the artist buried near his most well-known muse.

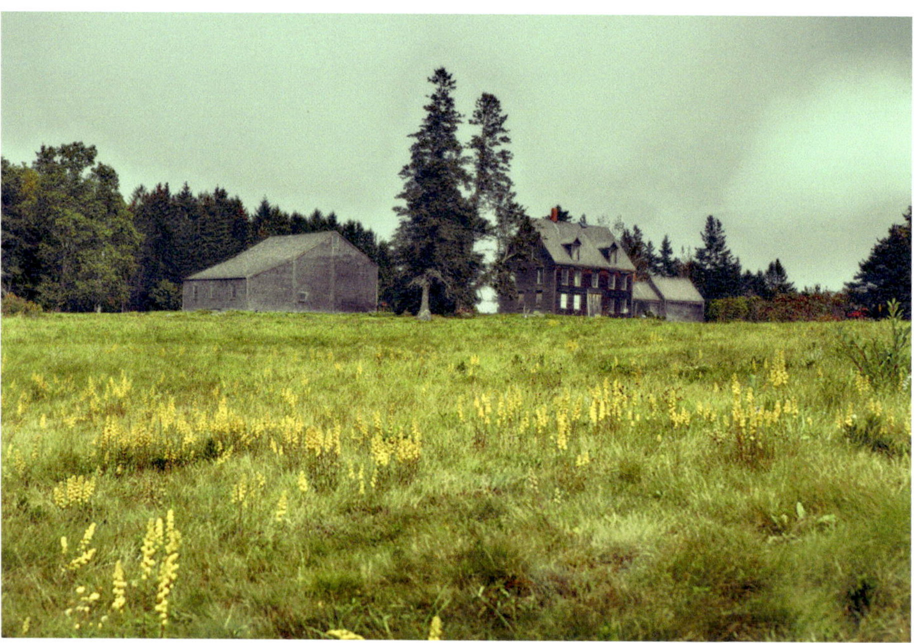

The view of the Olson house returning from the gravesites. Christina Olson was a proud woman who refused to use a wheelchair and it was when Wyeth observed her crawling across the field toward her house that he was inspired to create his most famous painting.

6

Ghostly Tales and Legends

The next five sections focus on graves or cemeteries in Maine that are attached to legends of the supernatural kind. There are many stories based here in Maine that challenge the imagination and defy reality, but what it is about these tales that causes them to endure the test of time?

It is difficult at best to pinpoint the exact time and place that a tale or legend begins. What is it about certain narratives that cause them to be handed down from generation to generation? These accounts become part of local lore and legend that strengthens as time passes, becoming preserved as though it were an actual historical occurrence. Often these stories are not questioned and become as real and tangible as the communities which created them.

That said, a word of caution is needed. Caution not to take information contained within the legends too literally, and always consider legends with a grain of salt. Somewhere between fact and fiction, legends reside.

Jonathan Buck

Jonathan Buck was the founder of the town of Bucksport and an important figure of Maine's historical waterfront along the Penobscot River.

Born 1719 in Haverhill, Massachusetts, Buck did not move to Maine until 1763 when he and his family sailed his sloop *Sally* from Haverhill to the mouth of the Penobscot River. They arrived at what was then known as Plantation No. 1, where Buck built a sawmill, the town's first general store, and he was appointed to the 5th Regiment of the District of Maine Militia in Lincoln County. As a Patriot, he was given a post as colonel at Fort Pownall located at the mouth of the Penobscot River. During this time, he was one of the leaders of the ill-fated Penobscot Expedition from July–August 1779. The expedition was the biggest naval operation of the Revolutionary War, and our country's largest naval defeat until the attack on Pearl Harbor 162 years later. The colonial forces saw losses totaling nearly 500 in casualties, captures, or maimings. After the expedition, Buck hid his wife and daughter in the nearby town where present-day Brewer is located before the British Navy destroyed Plantation No. 1, sparing only those who swore fealty to the English Crown. After securing his wife and daughter, Buck allegedly walked 200 miles to Haverhill to join his sons.[1]

After the Revolutionary War, Buck returned with his family to Plantation No. 1 and began rebuilding. The waterfront community prospered and grew until its incorporation in 1792. When the town was incorporated it was renamed Buckstown in honor of Colonel Buck.

The town's founder, war hero, and family man passed away at the age of seventy-seven in 1795. On his gravestone, the following epitaph is inscribed:

> *No mortal flesh can e'er withstand*
> *The power of Death's impartial hand*
> *But each without resistance must*
> *Receive the stroke and turn to dust*

The town was once again renamed Bucksport in 1817, and in 1852, the great-grandchildren of Jonathan Buck erected a monument to the town founder, just a few yards from his gravesite. It was not long after the monument was dedicated when a strange stain appeared on the front of the stone. The stain appears to be the silhouette outline of a woman's leg and foot, and soon after the appearance of the ghostly leg, rumors began.

Growing up on the coast of Maine, not far from Bucksport, I can recall hearing stories of the ghostly grave when I was around the campfire at boy scout camp. There are several versions of the story, and perhaps the most common, and the one I grew up hearing, involved Buck's time as a justice of the peace and his condemnation of a witch.

As the story goes, Buck was a staunch puritan who presided over the trial of a woman accused of witchcraft and he ruled against her, condemning her to be executed. On the day of her hanging, the whole community gathered around to witness the curse she directed at her judge just before she perished:

Jonathan Buck, listen to these words, the last my tongue shall utter. It is the spirit of the only true and living God which bids me speak them to you. You will soon die. Over your grave they will erect a stone that all may know where the bones of the mighty Jonathan Buck are crumbling to dust. But listen! Listen all ye people—tell your children—upon that stone will appear the imprint of my foot, and for all time long, long after your accursed race has perished from the earth, the people will come far and near and the unborn generations will say, "there lies the man who murdered a woman." Remember well, Jonathan Buck, Remember well![2]

The curse, supposedly uttered by the condemned witch, was first published in *New England Magazine* in the September 1902 issue in an article written by James O. Whittemore. In the end of his story, Whittemore goes on to point out the discrepancy between Buck's lifetime and the era of the Salem Witch Trials. Although superstitions surrounding witchcraft and sorcery remained well into the nineteenth century, the witch trials ended in 1693. Buck was born in 1719 and he did not arrive in what is now present-day Bucksport until 1763. Further, several sources have noted that no one was ever executed for witchcraft in that area of Maine.

Whittemore's disclaimer at the end of his tale did little to quell the torrent he created when he cracked the dam with his story. The article was picked up by *The Republican Journal* out of Belfast in the December 1908 issue, and it continued to be passed along through the generations, ending up at my campfire sometime around 1977.

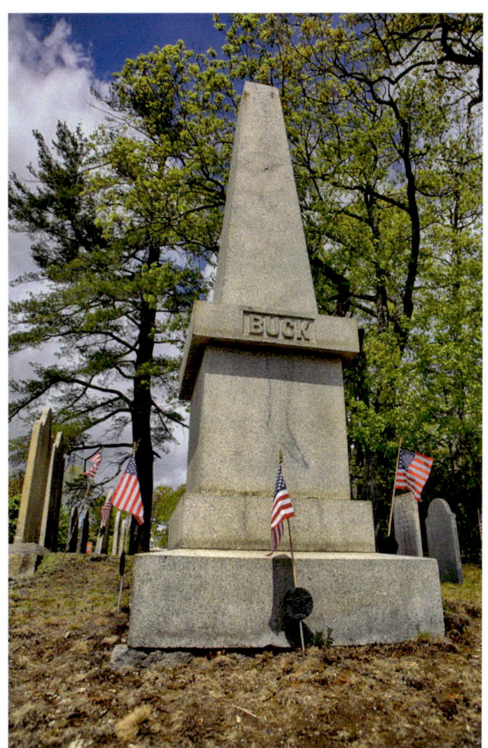

Right: In "The Foot of Tucksport," a 1939 long-form poem by Robert P. T. Coffin, the accursed witch ends her curse with the following statement: "And so long as a monument marks a grave of thine, So long shall my curse inscribe Thy tombstone with my sign!"[3]

Below: The Buck family cemetery sits along a busy highway, and it is fenced off to prevent visitors from entering the grounds. Judging by the treatment of other "witch sites" in Maine, this was probably a wise move to prevent desecration of the site.

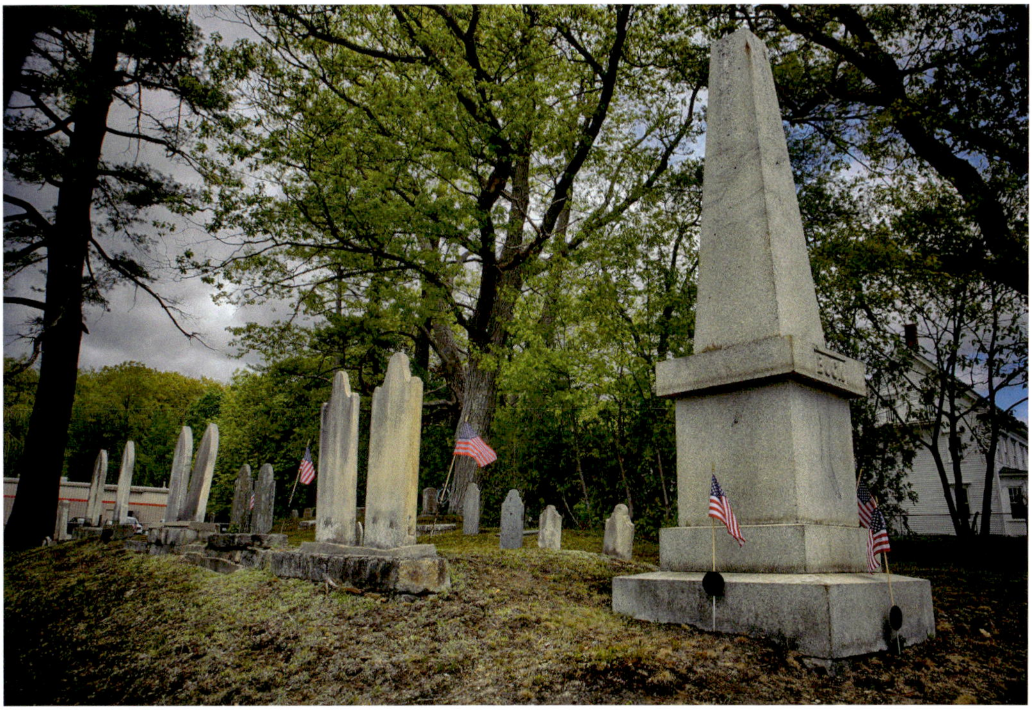

Although the legend of Jonathan Buck has endured the test of time, so too has the story of the revolutionary patriot and founder of Bucksport—an historic figure who should not be overshadowed by the legend.

The York Witch

Mary Nasson was a twenty-nine-year-old wife, mother, and some people say, witch. It is difficult to know if she practiced witchcraft, so we will have to contend with the facts and consider the legend.

Like usual, the legend varies, but the consensus is that Mary was a witch who died by something other than natural causes, some say executed. She was then buried on the outskirts of the burying yard and a stone was placed over her grave, as per town order, so that she would not escape.

Over the years, people have claimed to see the apparition of a woman helping children or picking flowers near the graveyard, but there has never been a report of anything malicious by this spirit who some claim is Mary.

Mary was born fifty-two years after the Salem Witch Trials had ended, but that simply means the moral outrage that society felt toward witches had ended. It is unlikely that public opinion, stereotypes, or prejudices against certain societal types had gone away. Even in our contemporary society we still have people believing the world is flat, so we can be certain that there were still those who believed in witchcraft in the decades following the trials in Salem.

Among those people was Jonathan Sayward, a distinguished member of the community and wealthy merchant. Sayward was a deacon in the church and a respected authority within the town during Mary's lifetime. According to York historians, Sayward even expressed his belief in witches and witchcraft when writing to John Adams in his defense of the English monarchy.[4]

Mary was a herbalist and was known to perform exorcisms; a person might be forgiven if they concluded that Sayward suspected Mary dabbled in the black arts. It is also apparent that others made the same conclusions; in an article published in 1894 by G. A. Emery, the author claimed that he was given to understand there was a stone placed on the grave to contain a witch.[5]

We also should consider things with a mind's-eye toward the past, rather than a contemporary mindset. This was an era when women had no rights and communities were much more class structured during this time, meaning a wealthy merchant had much more authority in the community than simple farmers or laborers would have had. This was an era when people who did not perform well in a community were sent to town farms, and women could be condemned simply by conflicting with others in the community, or their husbands.

Speaking of husbands, Mary's husband was Samuel. He remarried a woman named Joanna and moved the children to Sanford in 1778, four years after Mary died at age twenty-nine of unspecified causes.

The only trace of Mary's husband left at the York burying yard is on the epitaph he commissioned to have engraved in Boston:

Here rests quite free from Life's
Distressing Care,
A loving wife
A tender Parent dear;
Cut down in the midst of days
As you may see,
But—stop—my grief:
I soon shall equal be,
When death shall stop my breath;
And end my time:
God grant my Dust
May mingle, then, with thine.
Sacred to the memory of Mrs.
Mary Nasson, wife of Mr. Samuel
Nasson, who departed this life
Augst. 28th. 1774
Aetat 29.

I found it curious that the author chose to state that Mary was "Cut down in the midst of days." This seems to imply a rather violent or traumatic end, and it stood out sharply to me when I read the epitaph.

The wolf-stone covering the grave seems to be the least damning of all the evidence. They were often used in early colonial graves, but those graves tended to be shallow. It is hard to say how deep the graves are in York. There are indications that other graves used to be covered with wolf-stones, but why leave only Mary's in place?

Whether it was believed she was a witch or not is irrelevant. It is certainly up to us to draw our own conclusions, but even if Mary was suspected to be a witch, and even if she in fact were a witch, she deserves to be at rest.

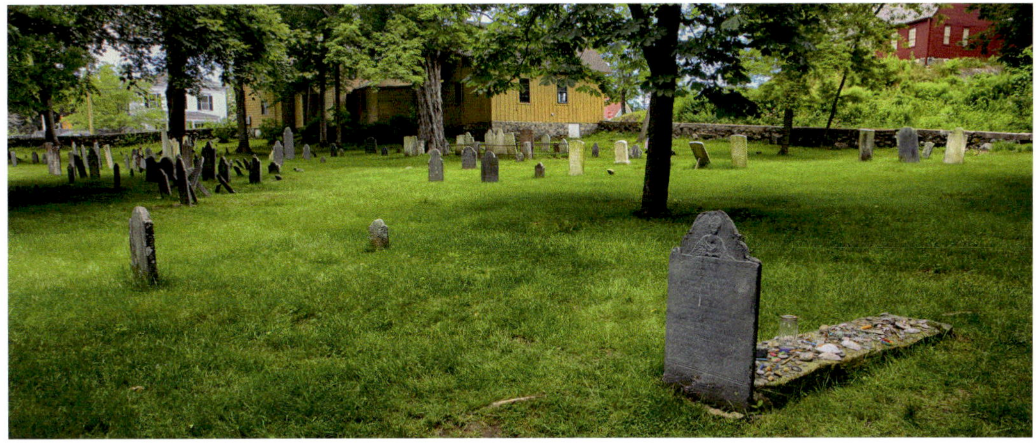

Mary's grave sits away from most of the graves and stands out quite prominently. Early town maps indicate other graves once had wolf-stones, but only this one remains. Early graves were often shallow and hogs or wild animals would dig up human remains if the stones were not used.

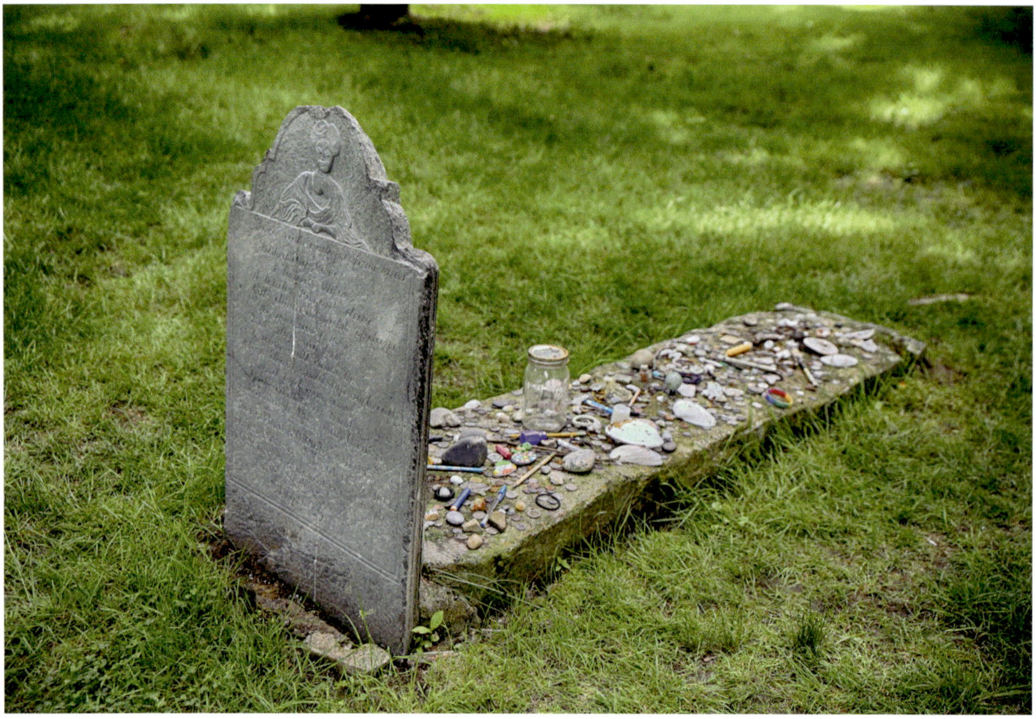

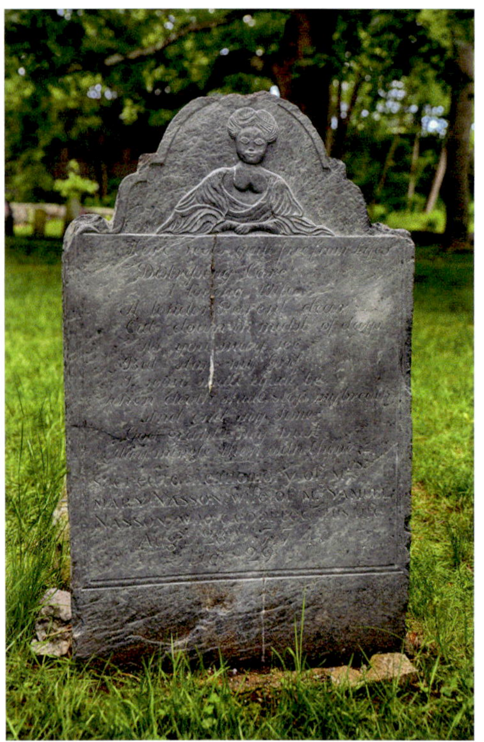

Above: Visitors and tourists continually pollute the grave with trinkets and unnecessary offerings. It is difficult to understand why some people would choose to mourn a gravesite in this fashion.

Left: Mary often has crows gathered around her gravesite and one left its calling card on her stone as I approached. Even though the crows only serve to exacerbate the witch rumors, Mary's inscription seems harmless enough, but there are curiosities.

Brown Cemetery

You are in such bliss; you have just closed on your new home in a community in southern Maine. You are out for your first evening walk around your new neighborhood with your best friend and faithful yellow lab, Bruce. As the sun sets in the neighborhood, you notice a ground fog settling in as the cool September air tries to overpower the last remnants of summer's heat residing on the ground. Your attention turns to the old cemetery that is in the middle of your neighborhood and a remnant of another time, you see two young girls playing around the cemetery. They are wearing white dresses, and they seem to be playing in the ever-darkening woods without a care. You do not recognize them as other children in the neighborhood and your maternal instincts take over as you walk toward the old graveyard to ask the girls if they need help.

Suddenly, Bruce abruptly stops. His hackles are up, and he begins to growl. For fear of frightening the girls, you turn and sternly tell Bruce to be quiet; as your attention turns back to the wayward girls, they have vanished, and the fog is enveloping the area where the girls once were, surrounding the graveyard with an eerie mist along the ground. You feel a chill and anxiously turn away from the graveyard with Bruce eagerly leading the way.

So goes the legend of Brown Cemetery, a small graveyard in southern Maine. The ghosts of two girls supposedly haunt this cemetery, and as the story goes, the two fell down a well or met with an unfortunate accident and now they can be seen playing or running about in or around the graveyard.

The local newspaper for the area states that according to legend the two girls were Mary and Catherine Chute, ages five and three.[6] The bodies of the girls were never recovered, but a memorial or stones were placed in the cemetery. Since the appearance of the apparitions, no one has been able to locate the stones, even though paranormal teams have looked.

It seems sightings occurred often in earlier years. There are stories of farmers tending nearby fields and seeing the girls playing in the cemetery. In recent years, sightings seem to have diminished. Perhaps it is just a lack of attention on the part of the modern observer. As I was there taking pictures on the roadside, the traffic was zipping right by and I doubt they even noticed me.

Aside from its spooky tale and nearby busy road, the cemetery is in a quiet, wooded neighborhood and is one of the oldest in town. It has some early settlement stones from the late 1700s, and it seems as though some quality slate was used for the stonework. Although there are no stones as magnificent as those found in the York Burying Yard, there are some excellent hand-carved slate stones here.

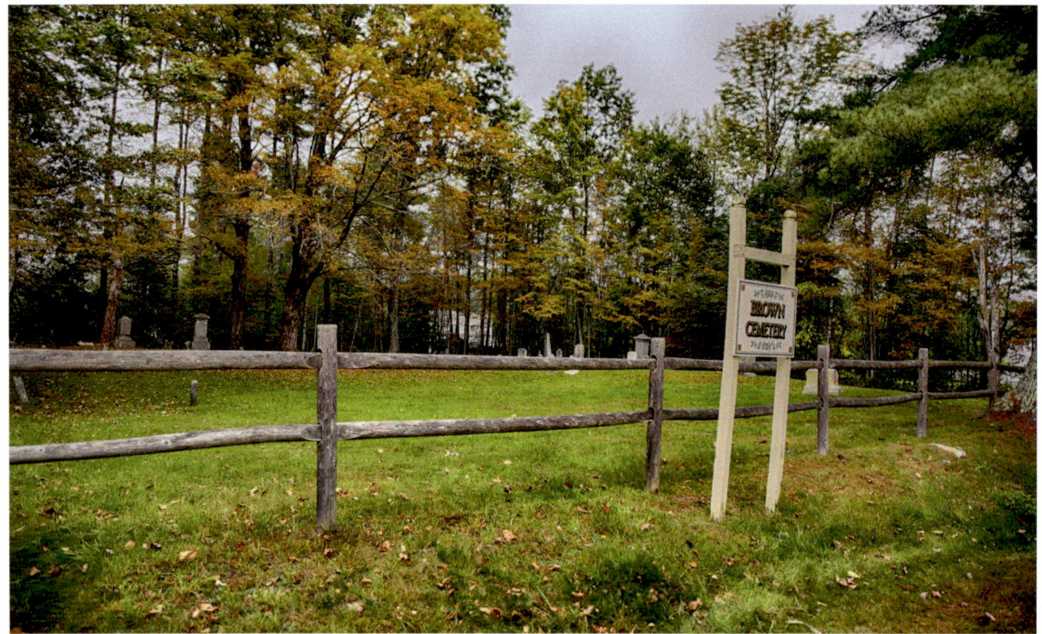

The Brown Cemetery as seen from the edge of the paved road. According to the local newspaper, it was along this road that a farmer first observed the apparitions as he was traveling in his horse and buggy.

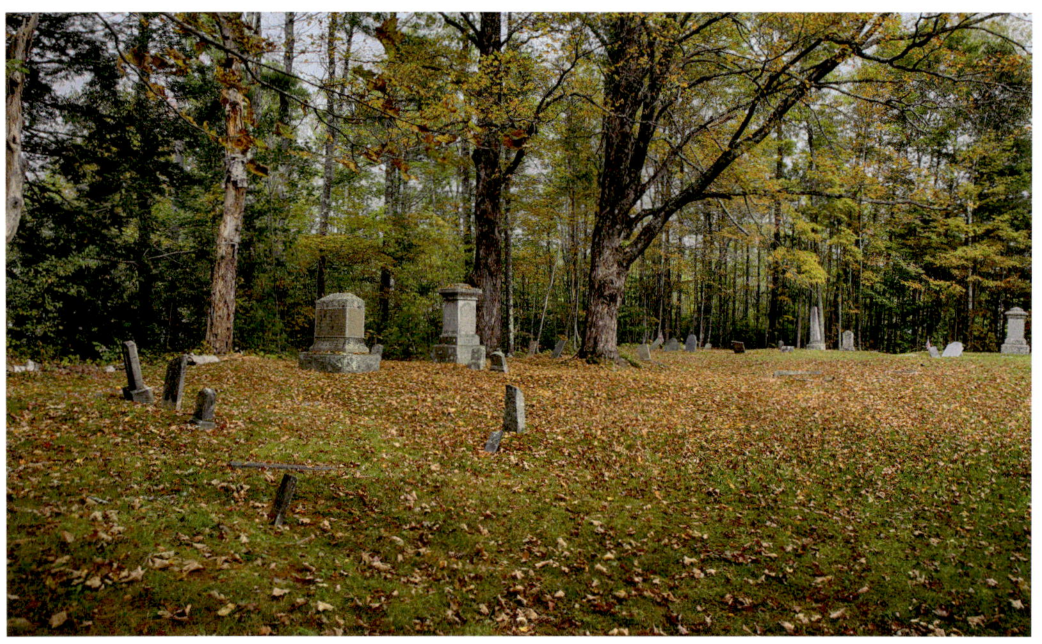

Looking from the road, this is the back left-hand corner of the cemetery where the ghostly girls are most often seen.

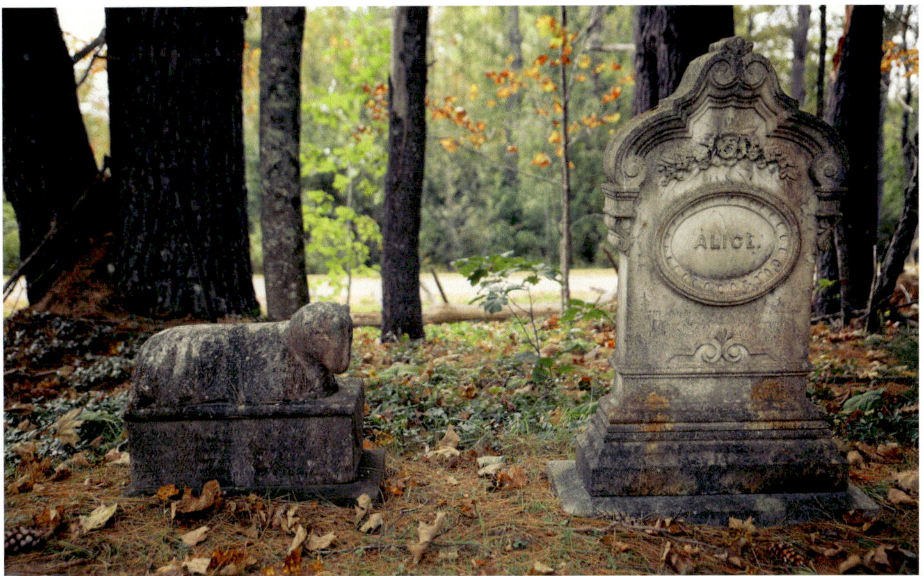

It is not difficult to understand why the ghosts of two children are seen in this cemetery, there are many children buried here. In the back corner of the cemetery, where the two spirits are often seen, these stones can be found. The lamb on the left is inscribed with a poem by Samual Taylor Coleridge: "Our darling little one has left us/ Ere sin could blight, or sorrow fade/ Death came with friendly care/ The opening bud to heaven conveyed/ And bade it blossom there."

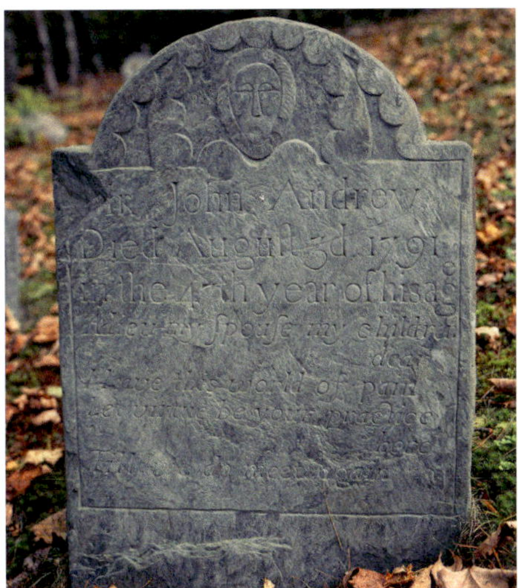

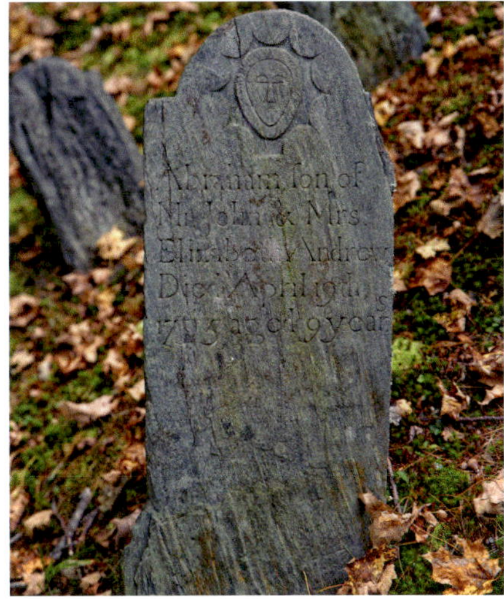

Above left: An early settlement stone in pristine condition. The stone is for John Andrew who died on August 3, 1791, at forty-seven years old. His stone is inscribed with the following: "Adieu spouse my children dear. I leave this world of pain. Let virtue be your practice till we meet again."

Above right: John Andrew's son Abraham died at age nine on April 19, 1795, nearly four years after his father's passing.

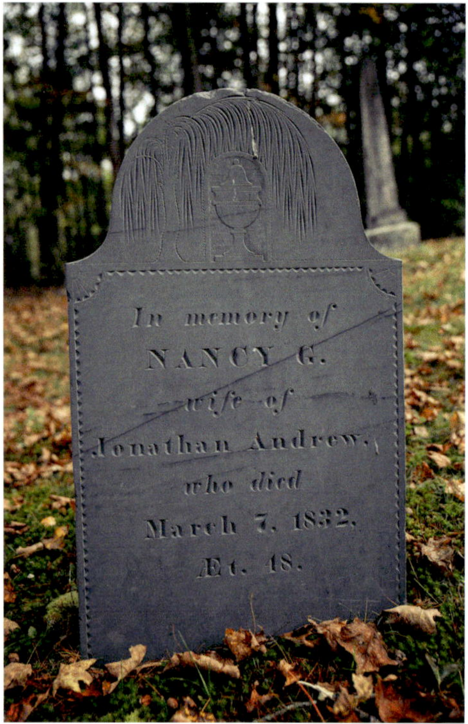

The death's head or angel of death carvings seemed to fall out of favor at the beginning of the nineteenth century when the willow tree came into use.

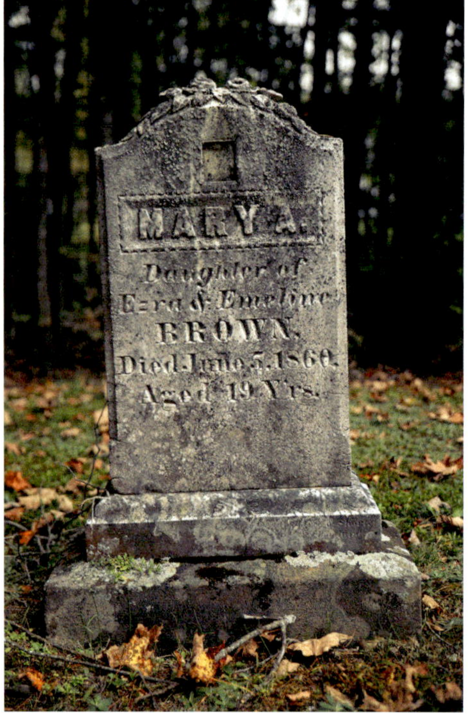

Mary A., daughter of Ezra and Emeline Brown, is buried in the family's namesake cemetery. Mary's stone appears to have had a portrait in it at one time. For a short time in the mid-1800s, some stones had small tintype portraits in them. I have only found one intact which appears later in this book.

Elizabeth "Lizzie" Lydston: The North Village Witch

Lizzie Lydston was a twenty-five-year-old woman who was married to a man named John. Not much is known about their relationship other than what can be found in records, and what can be found is somewhat disturbing. Four months after Lizzie's death in September 1869, John remarried a wealthy merchant's daughter named Jane in December and lived the remainder of his life in Auburn as a shoemaker.

It is difficult for us in the twenty-first century to understand the small village mindset of nineteenth-century New England. When we speak of "God fearing people" in our modern society, we do so as a tongue-in-cheek reference to a time in Puritan New England when people paid such a high reverence to The Almighty that they put to death those his did not share in their pious devotions; proclaiming offenders to be witches or accusing them of witchcraft, a label worn by people who, according to Puritans, walked in the very same league as the Devil. To be accused of witchcraft in the seventeenth or eighteenth century was a capital offense, and in the small village communities of the mid-nineteenth century, the mindset was not all that different from those of the centuries before.

What happened next is uncertain, but the legend is that Lizzie was dragged out of her home by villagers who then took her into the woods behind the North Church and hung her. They then buried her on the edge of church property.

But that is not where the story ends, and some may say it was only the beginning. As she was being bound, and the noose placed around her neck, she cursed the town and thanked them for bringing her peace, purportedly proclaiming:

Here me now for it has come to be
Now matter how you look, you shan't see
And the peace that you now grant to me
Shall evade you all, you'll ne'er be free

Now the church is gone and only remnants of its foundation remain; the village cemetery is the only thing that remains of the small church community, and as you walk around the graves, you will notice peculiar things. The tombstones are falling, broken, haphazardly placed, and the graves are becoming overgrown with tree roots encroaching on graves and swallowing gravestones. In some places, stones are lying on the ground, and in other spots, stones are broken. The cemetery seems to bring a general sense of chaos. There is no sense of peace and symmetry that you can usually experience and see in a cemetery. That is, until you see the grave of Lizzie.

Lizzie's grave is surrounded by a nearly perfect circle of cedar trees. Nothing at all grows inside of the circle of trees where Lizzie rests and there is an odd sense of calm when you visit the quiet cedar grove. As the legend goes, anyone who disturbs the peace inside of the circle is destined to meet with an unfortunate end, and local lore points to three young men who once disturbed the circle and each of them met an untimely demise. That said, I was unable to verify the deaths of three young men that would have been associated with this cemetery.

If you turn away from Lizzie's site and look back toward the main cemetery, away from Lizzie's solitary grave, you do not see the same calm, and the entire cemetery seems to be in a state of upheaval. It is as if peace has been taken from those interred there.

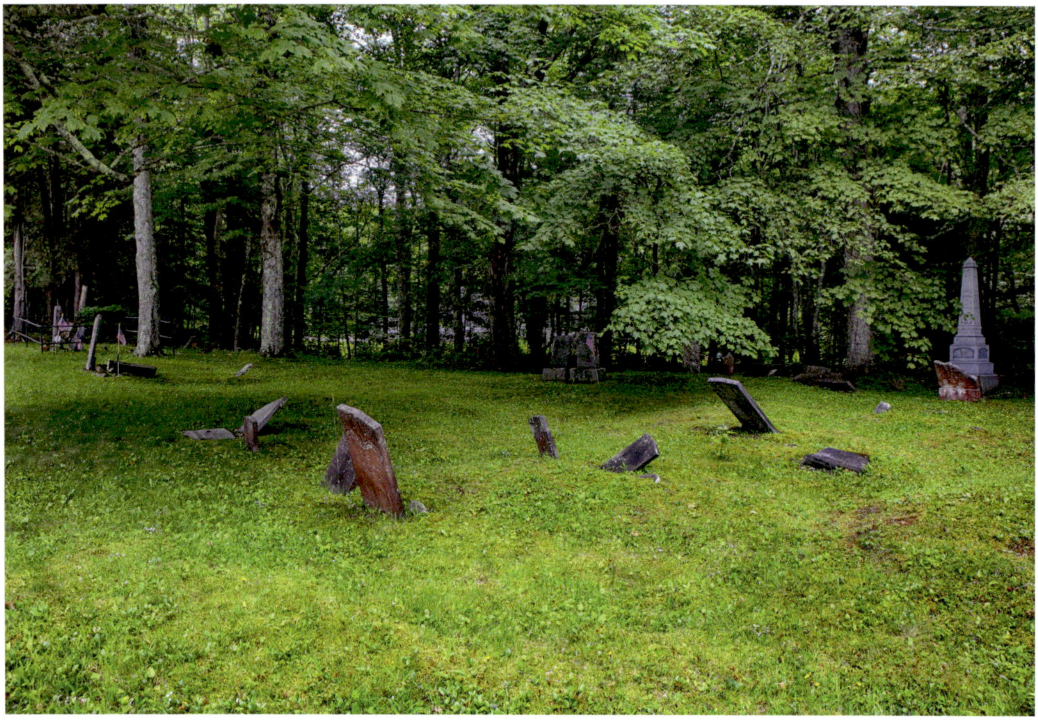

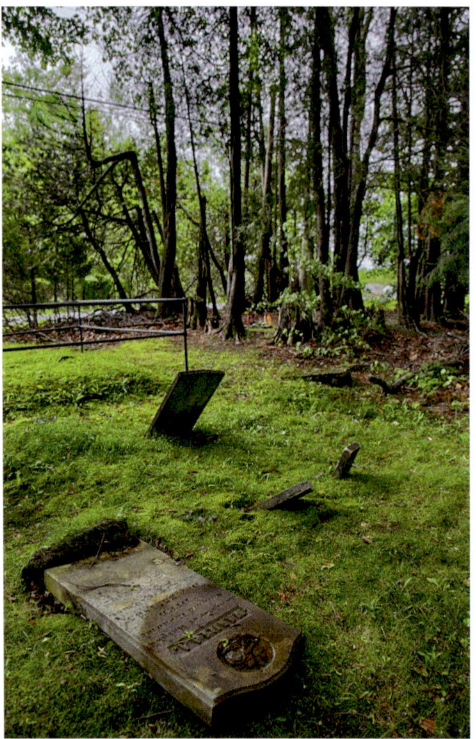

Above: Stones are broken, lying flat, strewn in opposing directions, and they leave the impression that everything was placed here haphazardly.

Left: Broken and misplaced stones are lying everywhere. Many are lying in opposing directions which seem to defy normal ground movements encountered in Maine.

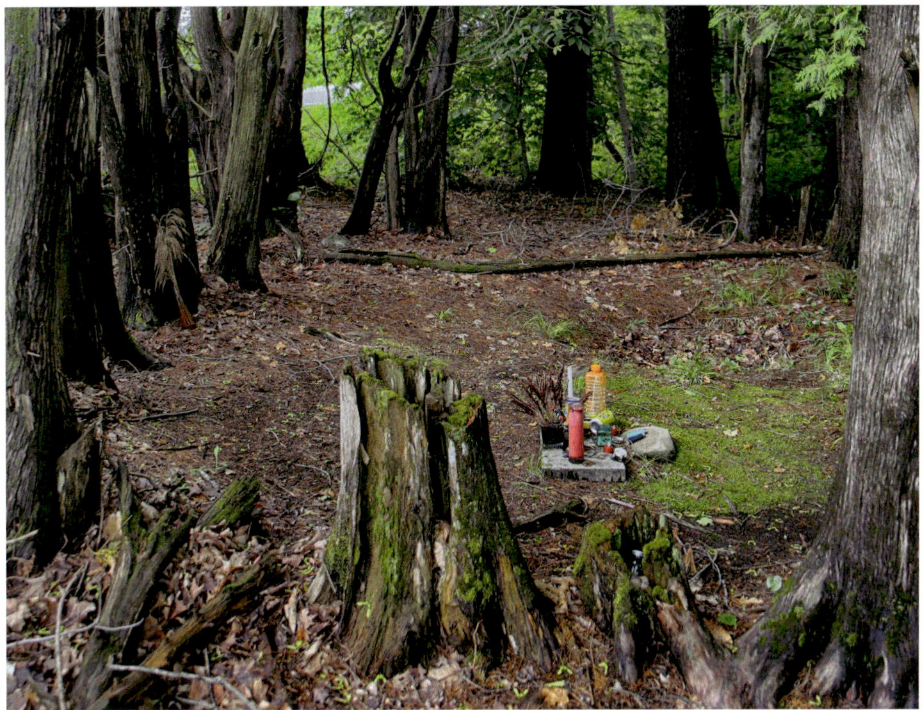

Above: Lizzie's burial site among the cedars. Nothing at all grows around the grave except for a couple of stray weeds.

Right: A strange and eerie sense of peace can be felt in the cedar circle where Lizzie is buried. Like the grave of Mary Nasson in York, visitors leave trinkets and offerings to Lizzie; this despite the legend that stipulates all who enter the circle are cursed.

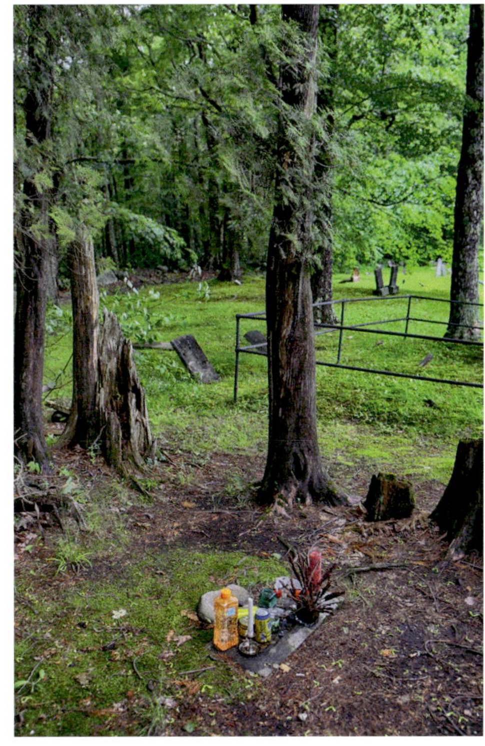

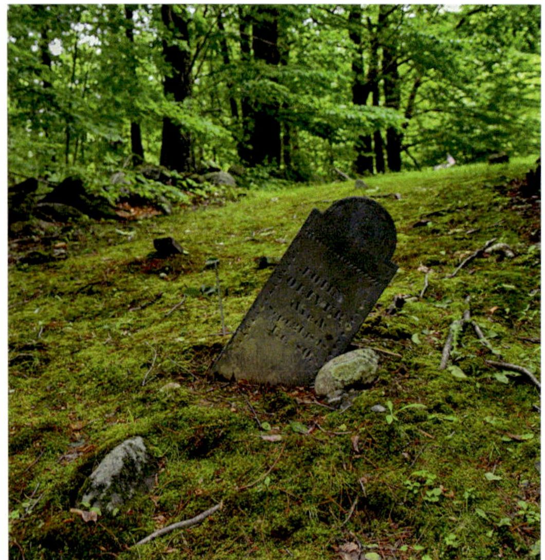

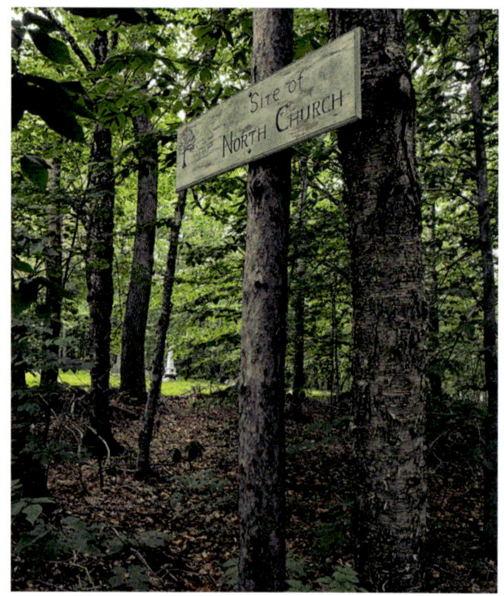

Above left: This stone is in the far corner of the cemetery, near the site of the North Church and opposite the grave of Lizzie. Like the grave of Lizzie, it is set apart from the others, but unlike Lizzie's grave, it has growth around it, and is in a state of decline.

Above right: Aside from a few foundation stones, this sign is the only evidence that remains to indicate that a church once stood here. Town records and historical documents reveal surprisingly little information about this village, its inhabitants, or its church.

The Smith-Anderson Burying Ground

According to paranormal groups, online ghost hunters, and even local newspapers, this cemetery continually ranks among the top ten haunted cemeteries in the state. Ghostly apparitions that roam the grounds, orbs, strange sounds, phantom voices, and even a strange knocking from within a large tomb have all been reported numerous times. Of all the things, perhaps the most curious are the reports of visitors having their vehicles disturbed while they were visiting the grounds. People have reported having their cars moved several feet, returning to find a previously locked car unlocked with the doors open, and even vehicles mysteriously stalling while approaching or leaving the site.

It is not difficult to ascertain why this graveyard has gained so much notoriety, it is a bit creepy. It is located off a rural road which turns onto a one-lane dirt road leading to the site. On the day I visited, wildfires in Canada were creating an ominous gray color in the sky. As I drove down the narrow-wooded road, I felt isolated, yet I did not feel alone.

As I walked around the grounds, I just felt as though I were being watched. I would hear random sounds, thumping or faint echoes in the woods which I attributed to neighboring activities even though the cemetery is quite far from any human activity.

Fortunately, my car was never bothered, and I saw no ghosts.

Aside from the spooky stories that surround this spot, it is worth the visit and has some wonderful early slate stones.

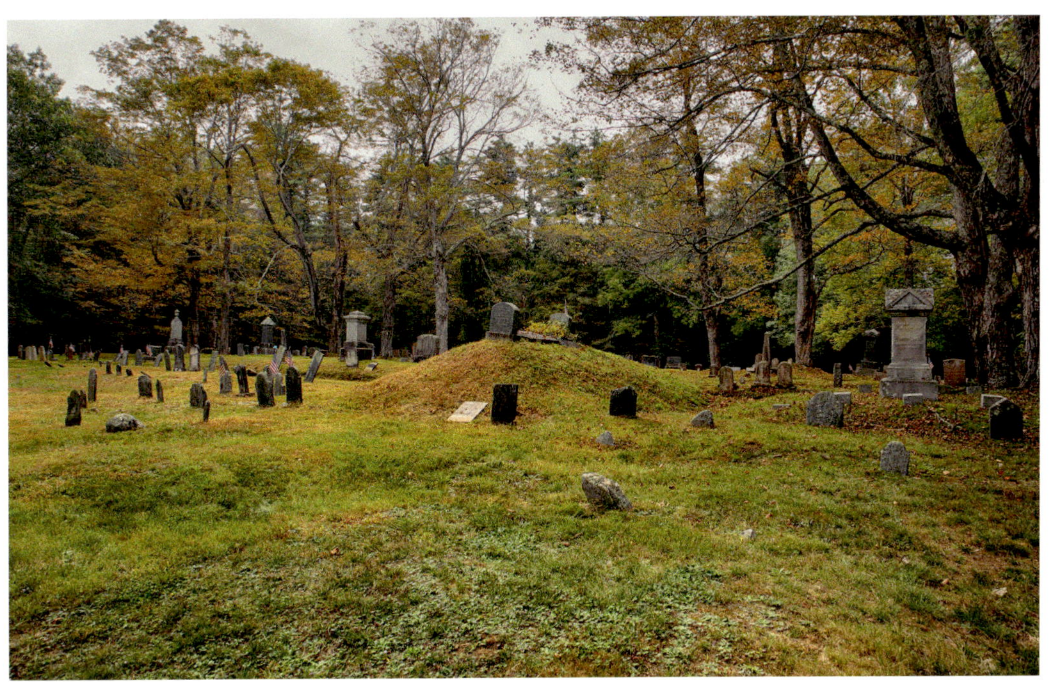

A wide shot of the burial grounds. It was impossible to shoot the entirety of this large cemetery with a very strange mound prominently in the center of the grounds.

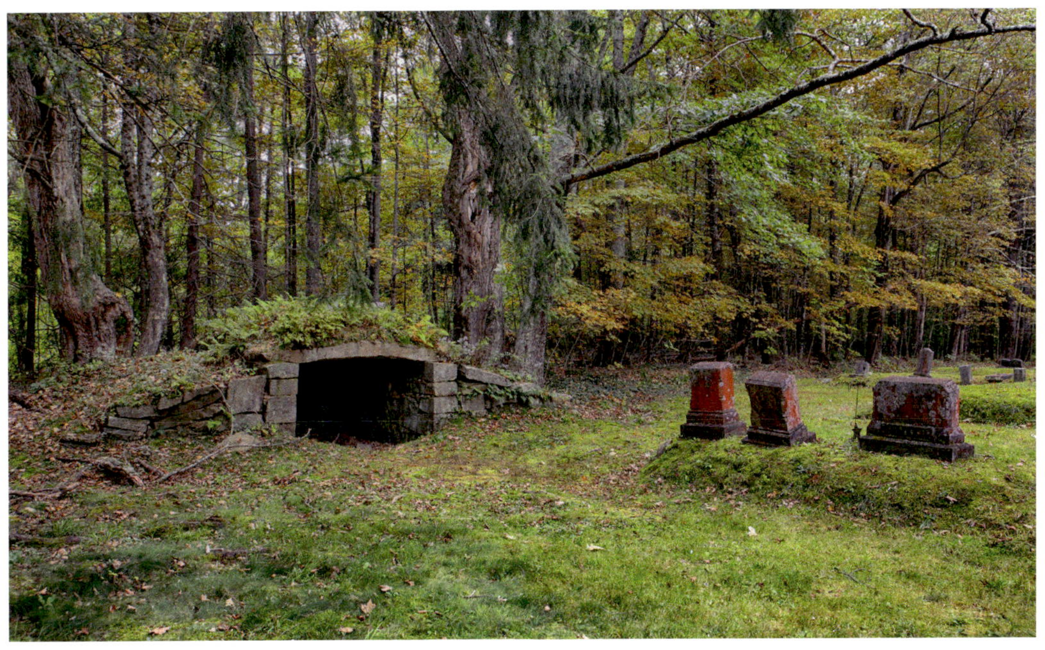

This appears to have been a holding tomb. According to paranormal blogs and local lore, this spot is occupied by a somewhat malicious spirit.

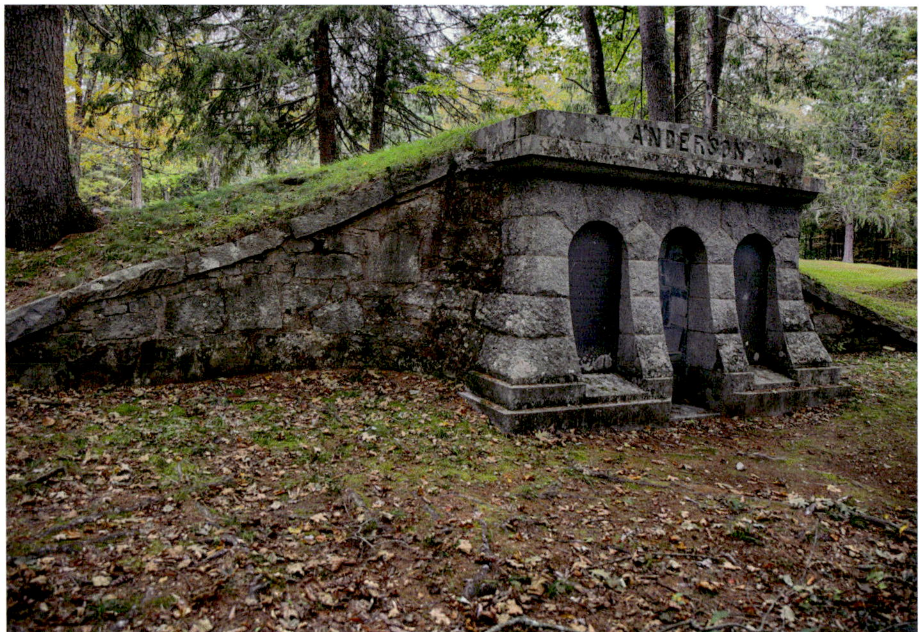

The Anderson family tomb. This location is also popular among paranormal thrill seekers and there are those who claim a knock on the vault's entrance will be returned by a knock from within; other stories claim that random knocking or thumping can be heard from inside.

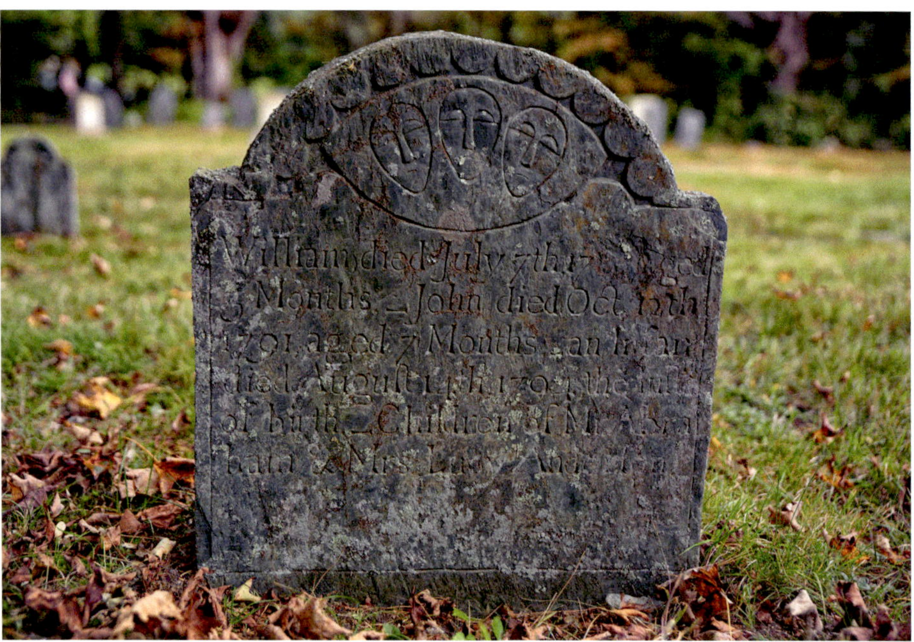

The three children of Abraham and Lucy Anderson. William died in 1790, he was three months old. John died in 1791 at seven months old, and the couple lost an infant at birth in 1794.

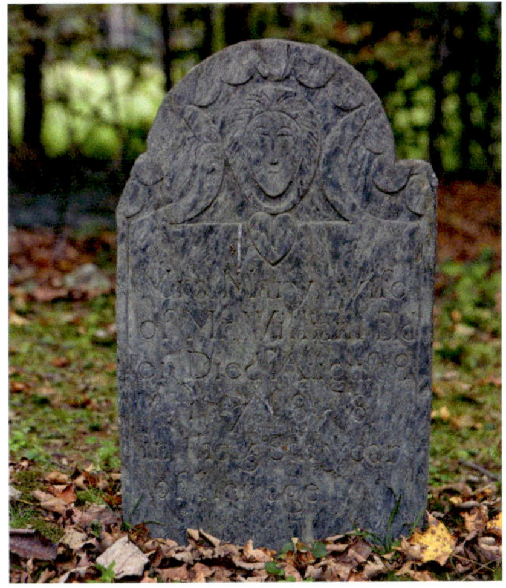 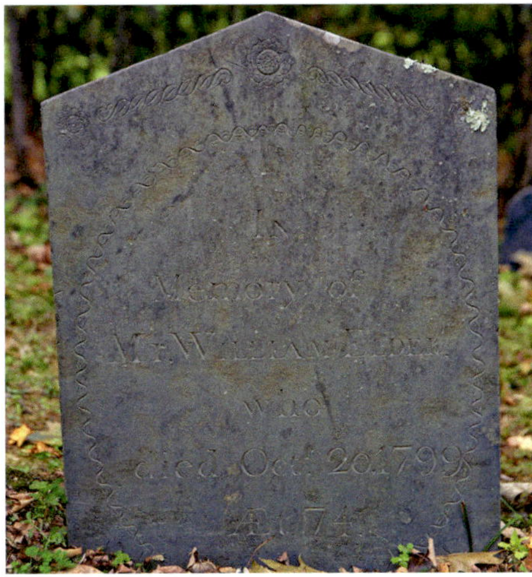

Above left: The carving in this cemetery has a distinct hand-drawn characteristic even though all stones were hand-carved during this period. This stone is at the grave of Mary Elder, wife of William. Mary died on August 8, 1788, at the age of thirty-eight.

Above right: Contrary to my statement in the previous image, the carving on this stone is very intricate with detailed scrollwork and flower designs. The lettering also appears much more planned out and measured. Although I am unable to confirm it, I suspect carvers with differing skillsets, perhaps traveling carvers were used at this site.

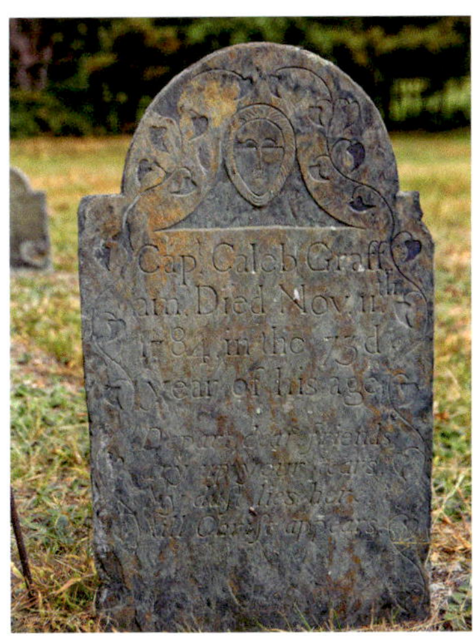 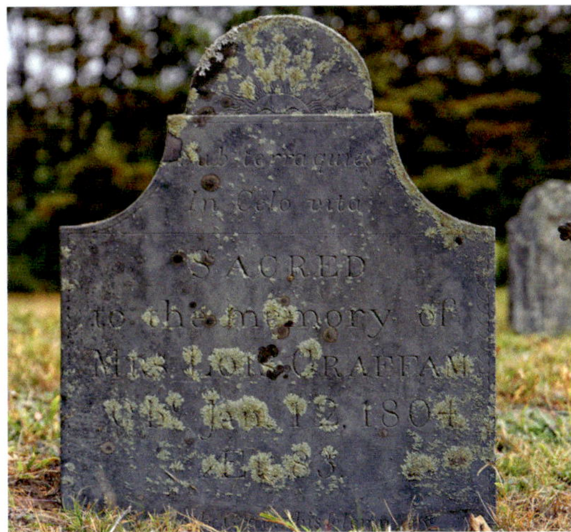

Above left: Captain Caleb Graffam died on November 11, 1784; he was seventy-three years old. On his stone is the inscription, "Depart dear friends dry up your tears. My dust lies here Till Christ appears".

Above right: Mrs. Lois Graffam's headstone bears the Latin inscription, "*Sub terra quies, In celo vita*" ("life under the earth rests in heaven"). She departed this earth on January 12, 1804, and at the bottom of her stone is the inscription, "Hark from the grave, this solemn cry."

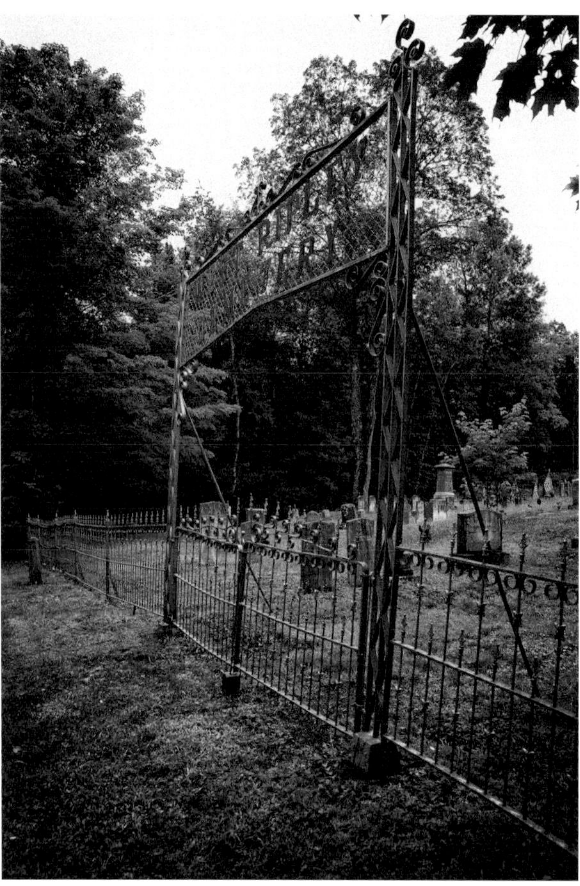

Cemetery Gate, West Ripley.
Image used to illustrate poem
"The Cemetery Gate."

The Cemetery Gate

*On a sunless evening, wind rustles through a willow tree as
a gate creaks; an ominous sound, like footsteps approaching
you from behind.*

*In the dimly lit cemetery, a ground-fog begins to circle
stone silhouettes. Then, from your eye's corner, a shadow
approaches: you turn but it is gone.*

*Suddenly all around, more appear. In every direction,
they are everywhere. Faceless shadows wandering aimlessly
and seemingly lost in the waning light.*

*You turn to flee, and in your fright, you are lost.
You realize then, the noise you heard was the caretaker,
closing the gate for you.*

7

The Notorious: Al Brady

Alfred James "Al" Brady was a career criminal and leader of the Brady Gang from 1935 until his demise at age twenty-six in 1937. He and his fellow gang members were responsible for over 150 armed robberies of banks and other businesses in a multi-state crime spree. In addition to multiple armed robberies, the crew also stole and highjacked cars, and committed at least two murders, Indiana state trooper Paul Minneman and twenty-three-year-old store clerk Edward Lindsay.

Sometime in early 1935, Brady met and befriended Rheul James Dalhover, a prospering moonshiner who was having difficulties procuring yeast for his whisky-making enterprise, a task which Brady helped with. Once Dalhover's operation was discovered and dismantled by authorities, Brady convinced Dalhover to embark on a career as a professional robber. With that, they embarked on a multi-state crime spree after recruiting third gang-member Clarence Lee Shaffer, Jr. The trio committed multiple robberies along with accomplice Charles Geiseking, heisting banks, jewelry stores, and even grocery stores. It was during the robbery of a grocery store in February 1936 when the gang killed store clerk Edward Lindsay.

Things seemed to be going well for the gang and they had always seemed to remain a step ahead of authorities, but on April 27, 1936, they robbed the Kay Jewelry store at Lima, Ohio, and their luck changed. During a shootout and their escape from the robbery, Geiseking was wounded by a bullet and his accomplices took him to a doctor's home in Indiana to be treated. The doctor alerted authorities and the ensuing gun battle resulted in the death of Sergeant Richard Rivers of the Indianapolis Police Department, but the gang averted capture. Then between May and September 1936, the gang and Geiseking were rounded up and arrested. Brady's gang was held for the murder of Sergeant Rivers and Geiseking was held for armed robbery, of which he was sentenced to ten to twenty-five years in the Ohio State Penitentiary. The remaining trio escaped imprisonment on October 11, 1936 when they assaulted a sheriff, stole his revolver, and hijacked an automobile with which they made their getaway.

Because the September robbery occurred in Ohio and the gang went to Indiana with the stolen goods, the crime suddenly fell within the jurisdiction of the FBI who promptly took up the trail of the three fugitives in October 1936. It was then that the trail went cold.

The gang had relocated to Baltimore and were living quiet lives undetected as they traveled to Indiana, Ohio, and Illinois to commit crimes. On May 25, 1937, after

47

robbing a bank in Goodland, Indiana, the trio encountered Indiana State Trooper Paul Minneman and Deputy Sheriff Elmer Craig: killing the former and wounding the latter. Brady and his gang's ruthless activities earned Brady the FBI title of "Public Enemy No. 1" and one of the greatest manhunts in this country's history began.

After some cleaver detective work and a tip from a local gun seller in Bangor, it was revealed that the trio had made multiple trips to a hardware store in Maine to obtain guns beginning in September 1937. It was then that a collaborative effort between the FBI, the Bangor Police Department, and the Maine State Police brought more than fifty officers to the city of Bangor in efforts to capture Brady and his gang.

On October 12, 1937, the gang was cornered in downtown Bangor where Dalhover was taken into custody by undercover officers once he entered the hardware store. Shaffer engaged officers in the street where he was immediately gunned down. Brady was killed shortly after exiting the stolen car he was in, and he also died in the street after a brief but spectacular shootout with the FBI. When officers disarmed the deceased Brady, they recovered Trooper Minneman's .38-caliber revolver from Brady's right hand.[1]

Dalhover was executed by electrocution at the Indiana State Penitentiary on November 18, 1938. Shaffer's remains were claimed by his family and Brady was buried in an unmarked grave outside of town in what was known as the city lot at Mt Hope Cemetery. The grave remained unmarked for seventy years until 2007 when a reenactment of the shooting and a graveside service resulted in Brady receiving a proper burial marker.[2]

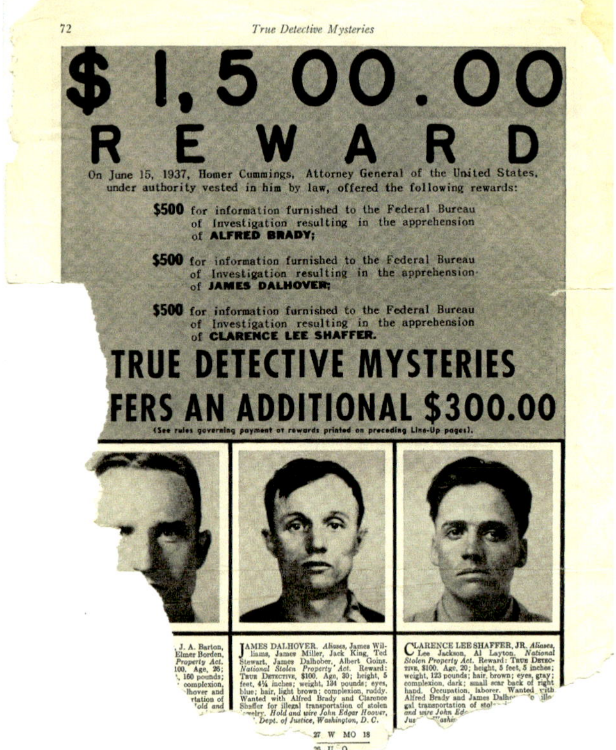

The reward poster published by *True Detective* magazine in which a $500.00 reward was offered for each member of the Brady Gang. The reward was given to Everett "Shep" Hurd, the store owner in Bangor who alerted authorities.[3]

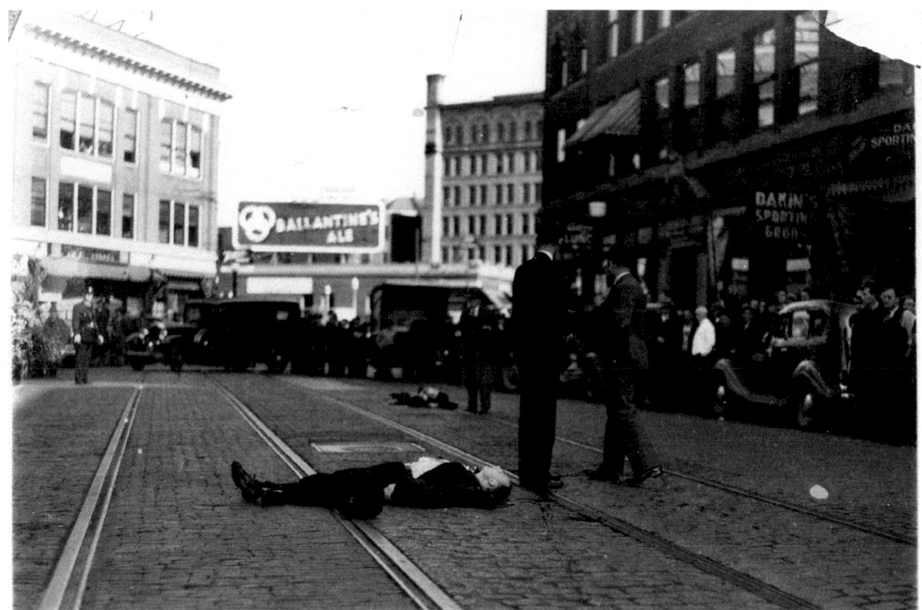

A view of Central Street in Bangor after the shooting occurred. Brady is lying in the foreground and Shaffer is lying back and to the right. A crowd has gathered around and only officers and FBI agents are near the deceased.[4]

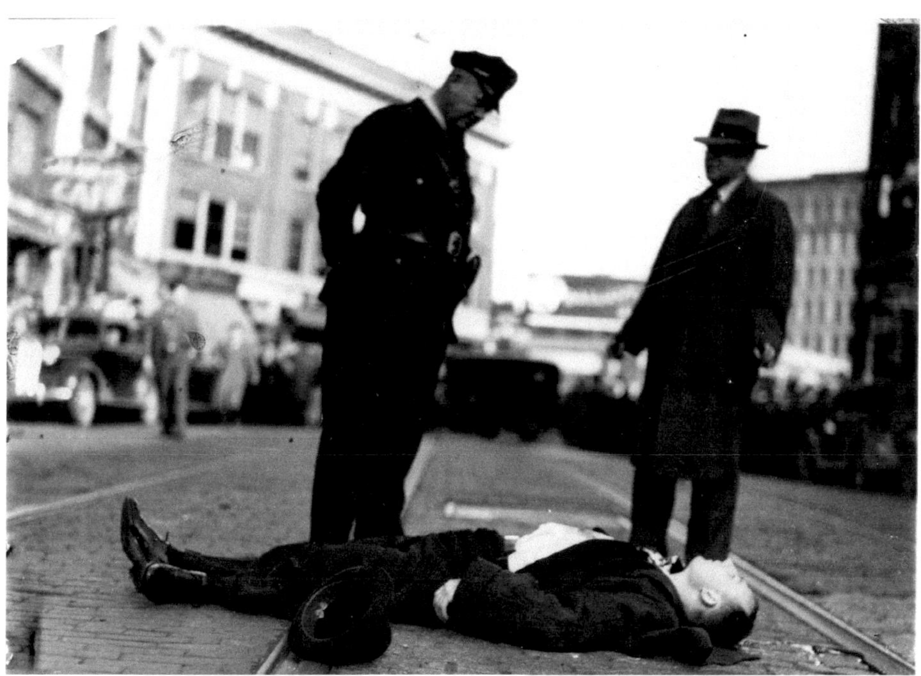

Al Brady lying dead in the street as a Bangor police officer looks on while an FBI agent discusses the day's events.[5]

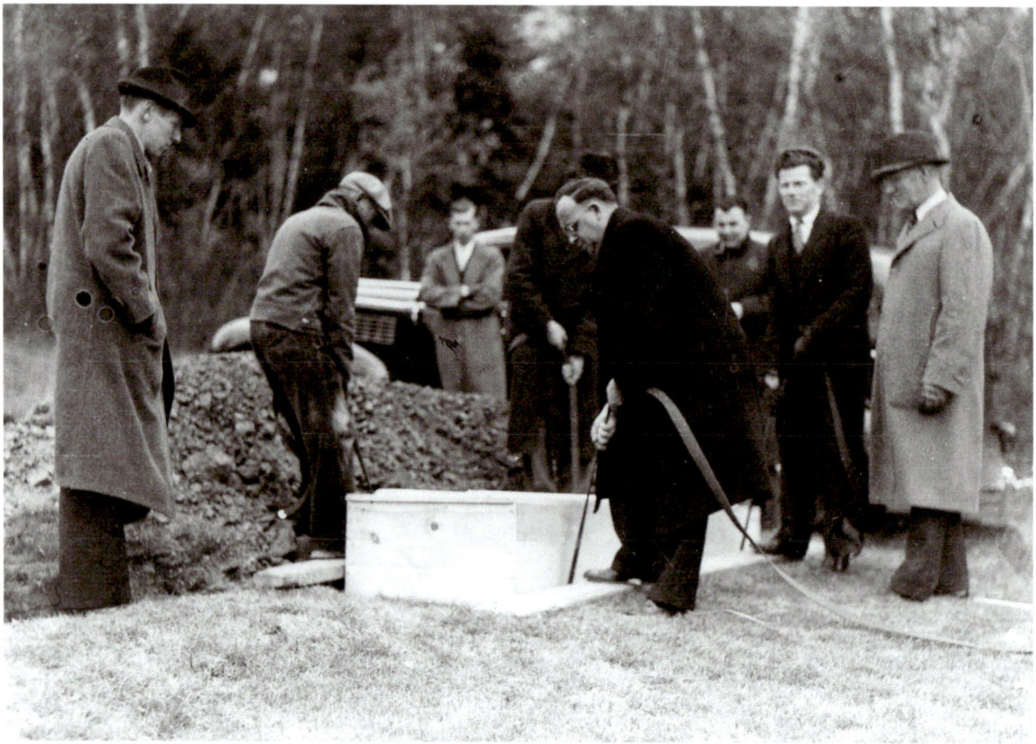

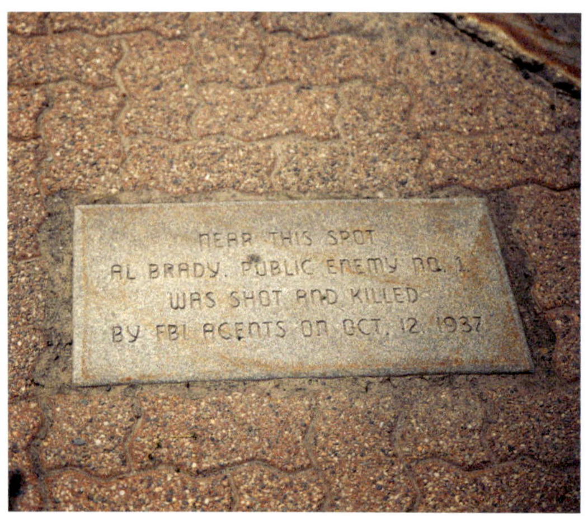

The pine box containing Brady being lowered into a soon-to-be unmarked grave in the far corner of the city lot at Mount Hope Cemetery.[6]

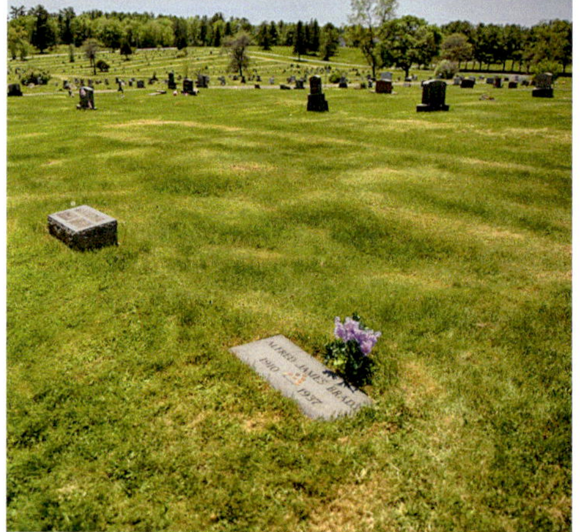

Above left: This plaque commemorates the location where Brady and his gang were approached by the FBI and the shootout occurred in downtown Bangor.

Above right: Brady's grave is now marked, and he has more company now that the city lot is being used as a more functioning part of the cemetery.

8

The Heroes: Some Gave All

Originally, I was going to use this chapter to talk specifically about Maine's war heroes (such as Medal of Honor recipient Major-General Joshua Chamberlain; 1828–1914).

However, I believe Major-General Chamberlain would forgive me if, rather than discuss the biography of one or two heroes interred in Maine, I use this space to honor all our heroes from all our nation's wars. Without them, we could not enjoy the freedoms that we often take for granted. Freedoms such as reading or writing this book.

Please join me in remembering our nation's fallen; from the major generals who helped forge our nation, to the privates who died during their first hour in battle, we salute you all and thank you for your service.

In remembrance, here is the list of United States conflicts and the year of conflict resolution.

The American Revolution, 1783
War of 1812, 1815
Indian Wars, 1898
Mexican War, 1848
Civil War, 1865
Spanish-American War, 1902
Worl War I, 1918
World War II, 1945
Korean War, 1953
Vietnam War, 1975
Desert Sheild/Desert Storm, 1991
Global War on Terror, unresolved[1]

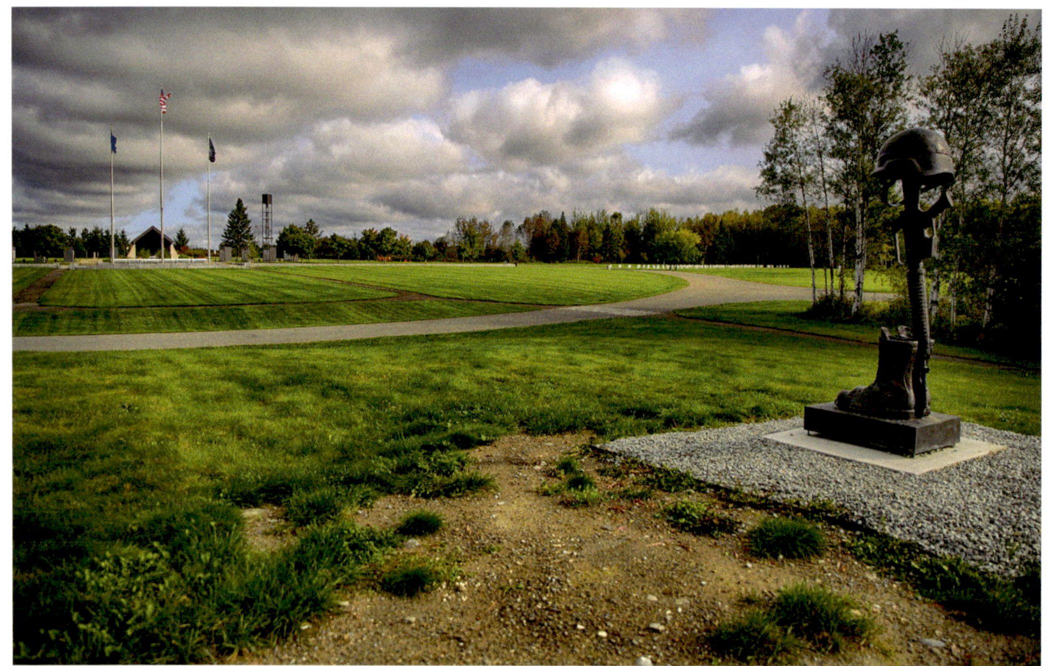

An early morning view at the Northern Maine Veteran's Cemetery. This relatively new cemetery in Aroostook County sits on 34 acres in the city of Caribou. The cemetery was dedicated in June 2003 and has the capacity to hold over 10,000 interments.

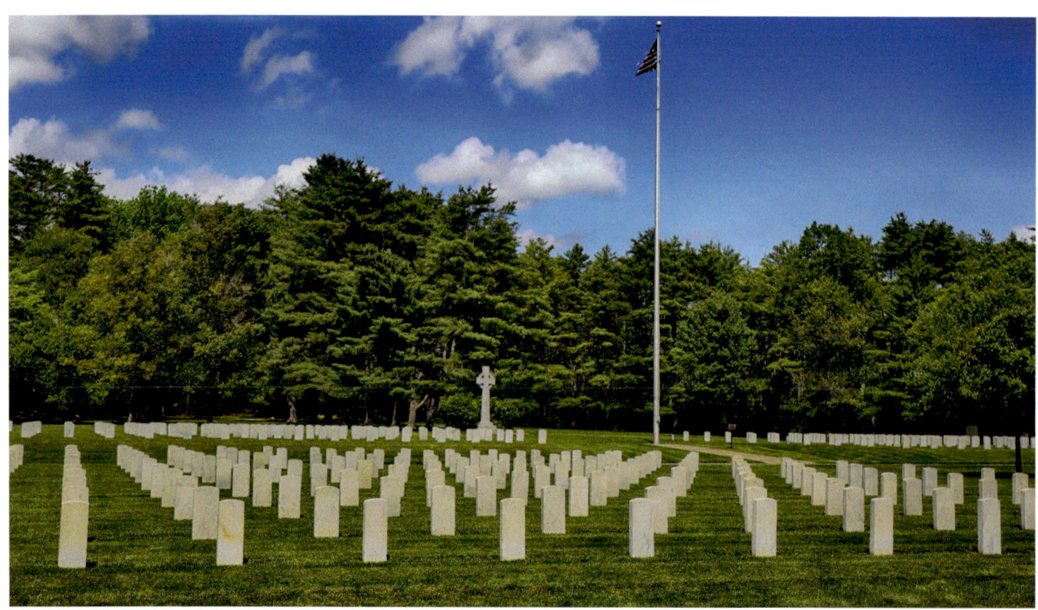

The United States Department of Veterans Affairs, Togus National Cemetery in Togus, Maine. This cemetery has been closed to new interments since 1961 and has more than 5,200 interments.

9

Eternally Yours

In 1983, I was a junior in high school at a basketball game when a freshman girl walked into the school and I saw her for the very first time. It was then that I knew, without reason and without argument, she was the one. Suddenly, there was no other human being on the planet that interested me more, and she became the most important person in my world.

Fast forward to now, 2023; she remains the most important person in my world, we have made a life together, raised a daughter, and have grandchildren now. I could not imagine being with another person, and if one were to subscribe to the concept of a soulmate, I believe she would meet the criteria.

"To have and to hold … until death do us part."

Marriage vows vary depending on religious denomination, or belief structure, but the gist remains the same. It is a commitment two people make to one another, pledging to experience the trials and tribulations of life together, enduring both the bad and the good without wavering in the commitment that is the foundation of their relationship.

Monogamy is arguably a religious concept, and many believe that monogamy in humans separates us from the beasts in the field, but the concept of eternal love, the soulmate, goes far beyond the physical and becomes more of an existential connection.

As humans, we have an extraordinarily broad range of interests and passions that creates a great diversity within the human condition. We all have different pursuits of happiness, and we all respond differently to external stimuli; in short, no two humans think or feel exactly the same way. We each have different views on religion, philosophy, politics, even the way in which we live our lives differs from individual to individual. When we select our social groups and formulate relationships, we tend to find those who share common interests and they become "our people."

For a lucky few, the similarities form a bond and their commonalities become so compatible, they overcome any adversity together. That is, any adversity except death. Often, when two people dedicate their lives to one another, the grief becomes too great and even death cannot keep them separated for long.

This chapter is dedicated to those who feel we can be bound to one person, not just for life, but throughout all eternity in a bond of souls.

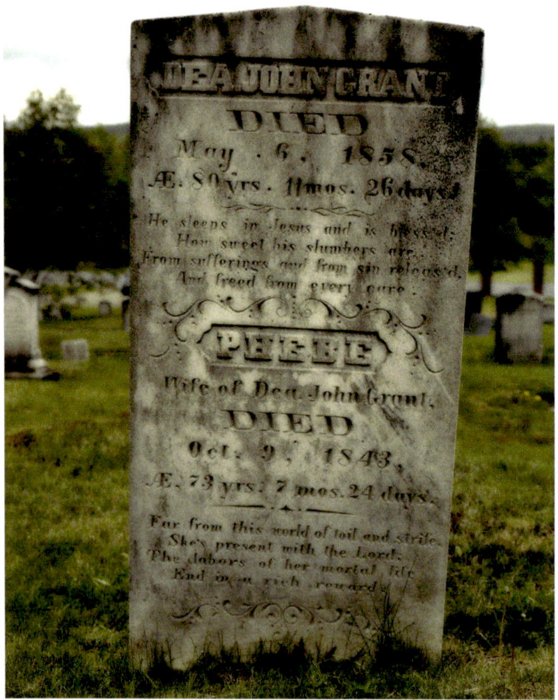

Deacon John Grant and his wife, Pheobe, died 180 years ago and their joint gravestone still reads clearly as though it were recently carved. There is no need for me to put the information in the caption.

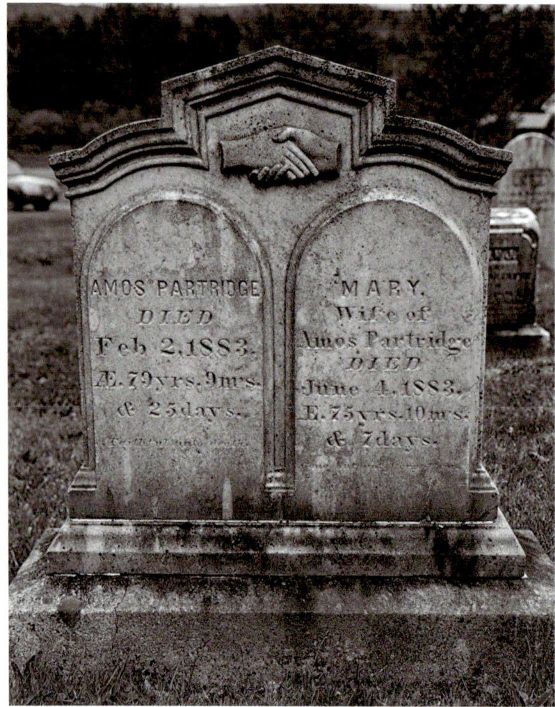

Amos and Mary Partridge both died in 1863. Amos was seventy-nine and his epitaph reads, "Faithful unto death." Mary was seventy-five and her epitaph reads, "Gone, but not forgotten."

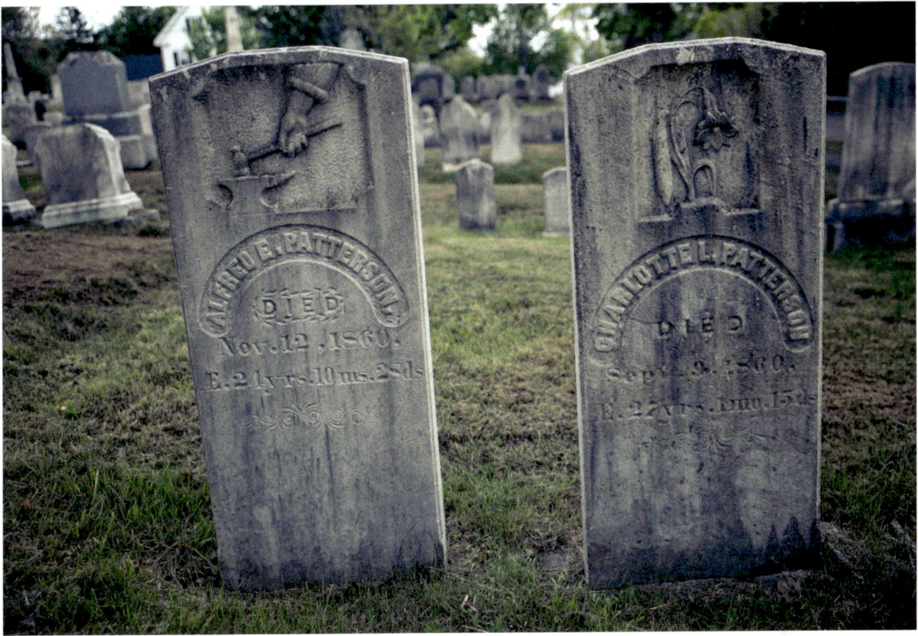

Charlotte outlived her husband, Alfred, by two months and two days. He was twenty-four years old and she was twenty-seven when they both died in 1860.

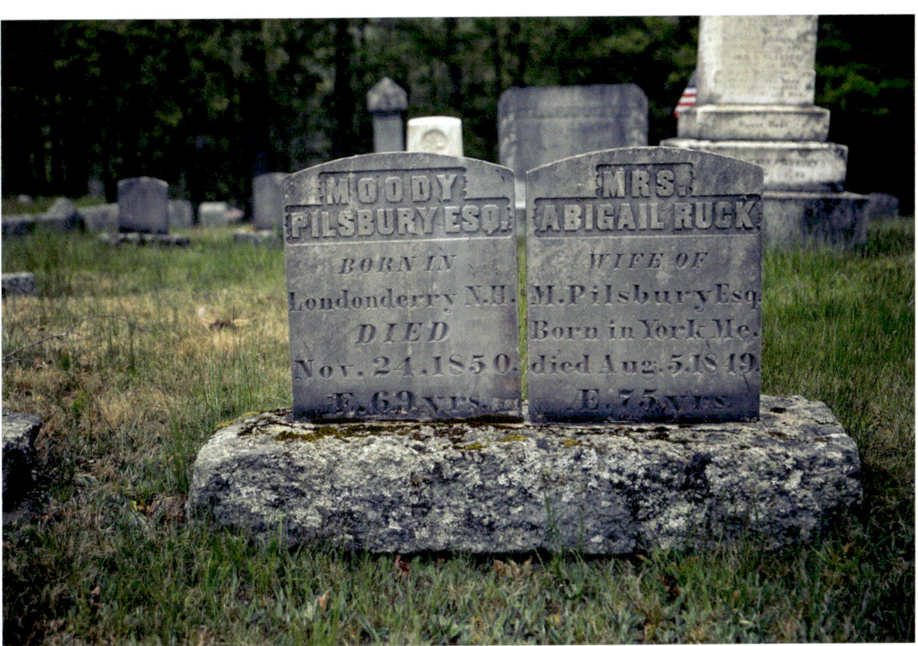

The Pilsburys died fifteen months apart from each other, and I really wanted to include this photo in the book because the stone the markers sit upon seems to symbolize the solid foundation their relationship was built on.

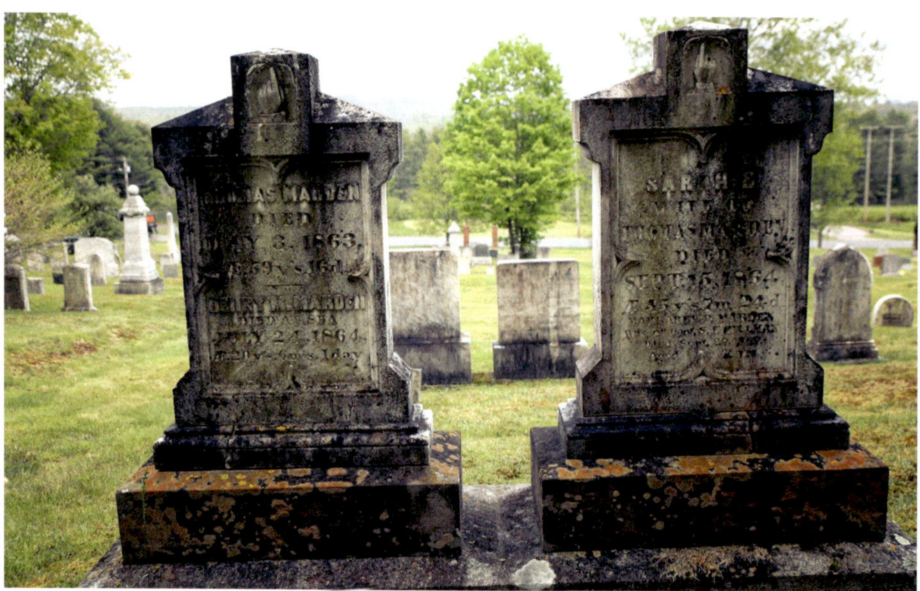

Love and loss: Sarah B. Marden lost her husband, Thomas, in May 1863 and their twenty-year-old son, Henry, died at sea fourteen months later, on July 24, 1864. Almost two months after Henry was lost, Sarah followed them both on September 15, 1864; she was fifty-five years old. The couple's daughter, Margaret Marden, died at thirty-one on September 29, 1867.

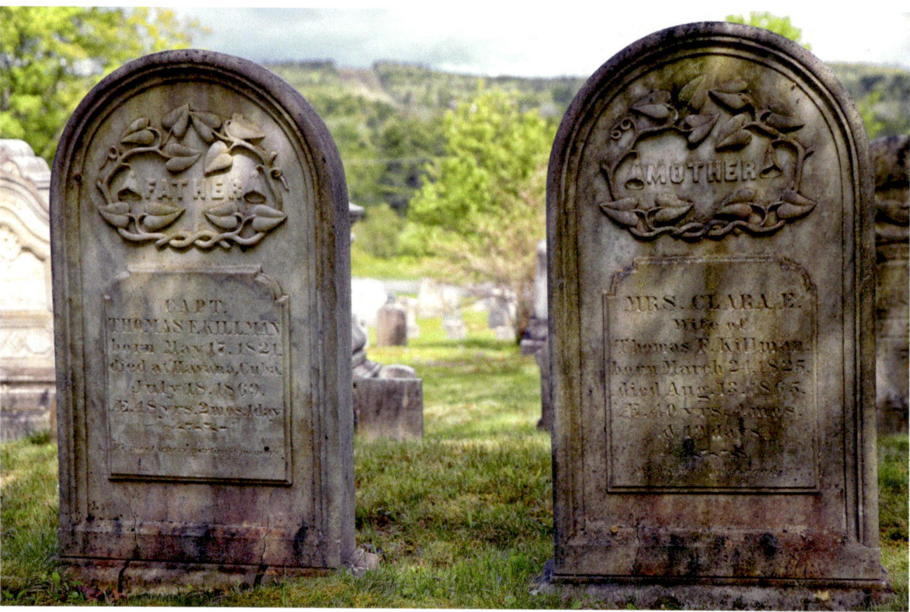

Captain Thomas F. Killman died in Havana, Cuba, on July 18, 1869, in his forty-eighth year. His stone is inscribed with, "We meet where parting is no more." His wife, Clara E. Died, on August 13, 1865; she was forty years old. Her stone is inscribed with, "We part to meet again."

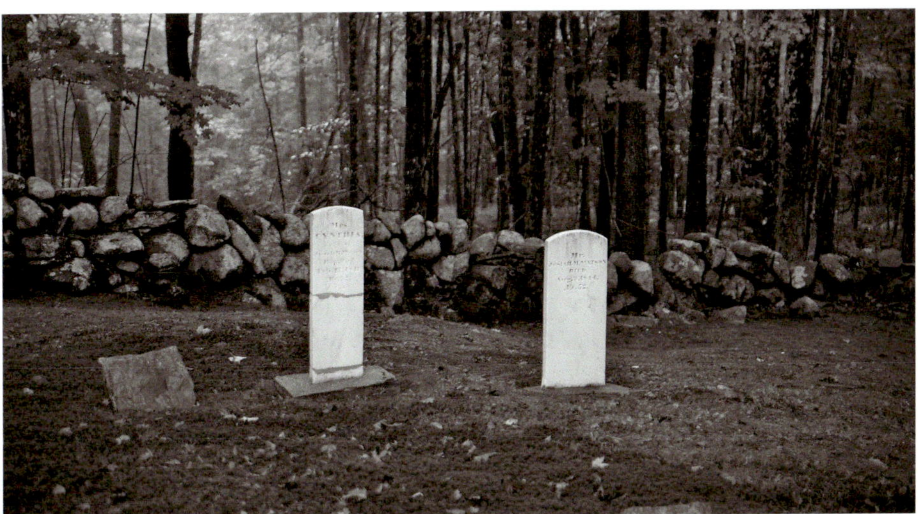

There is something about this photo that is eerie. I took it on a very damp and foggy morning and these stones had a surreal glow about them and stood out above all the others in the cemetery. The stones are very plain yet very distinct, and I feel as though the couple really wanted to make sure I noticed them at the very back of the poorly lit cemetery. The couple is Josiah and Cynthia Watson who were both fifty-two years old when they died almost exactly six months apart in 1841. Not much else is known or revealed in the records.

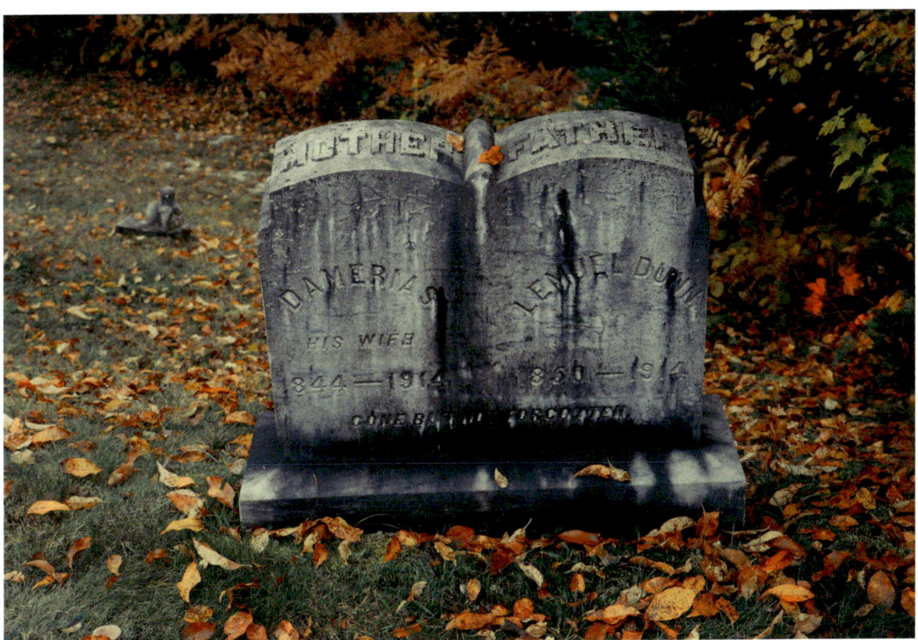

All that is known of Damerias and Lemuel Dunn is that they were a mother and father, and they both died in 1914. Their stone is inscribed with "Gone but not forgotten."

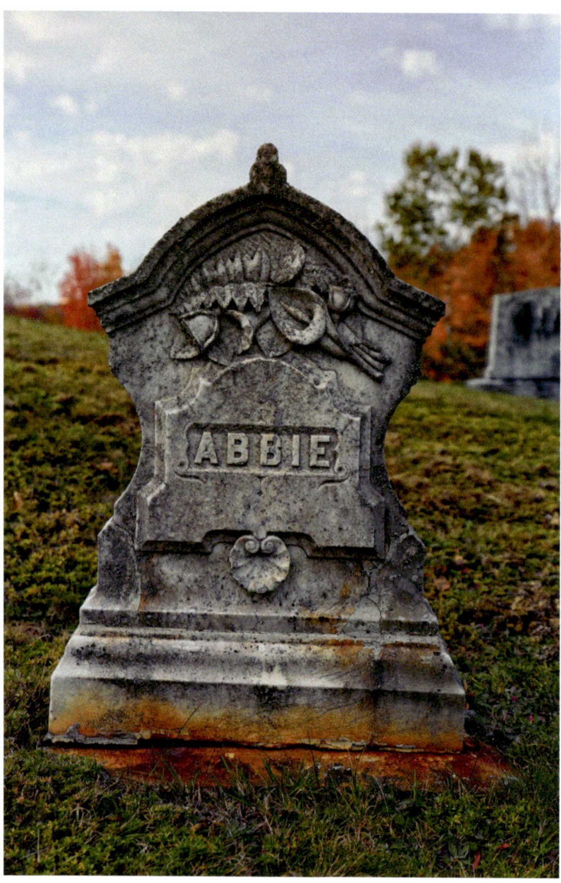

The grave of Abbie at
Mount Pleasant Cemetery in
Cambridge. Image used as
illustration for poem "At Rest."

At Rest

My beloved has gone away
She now rests on yonder knoll
All the things I wish to say
are said to a grass veneer

Time goes on, it takes its toll
bringing change each passing year
and it pains me to my soul
to come and visit her here

10

Little Lambs

There are few things worse for a parent to endure than the loss of a child. There are literally no words that can express the grief and sadness a parent experiences with the loss of their progeny. To provide a sense of closure and make sense of the profound loss a parent feels, gravestones and markers are erected to memorialize their children. The markers are as unique as the young lives which were lost.

Mother

A mother mourns a child stillborn
or one who dies old and gray
A daughter or son can't be undone
She'll grieve till her dying day

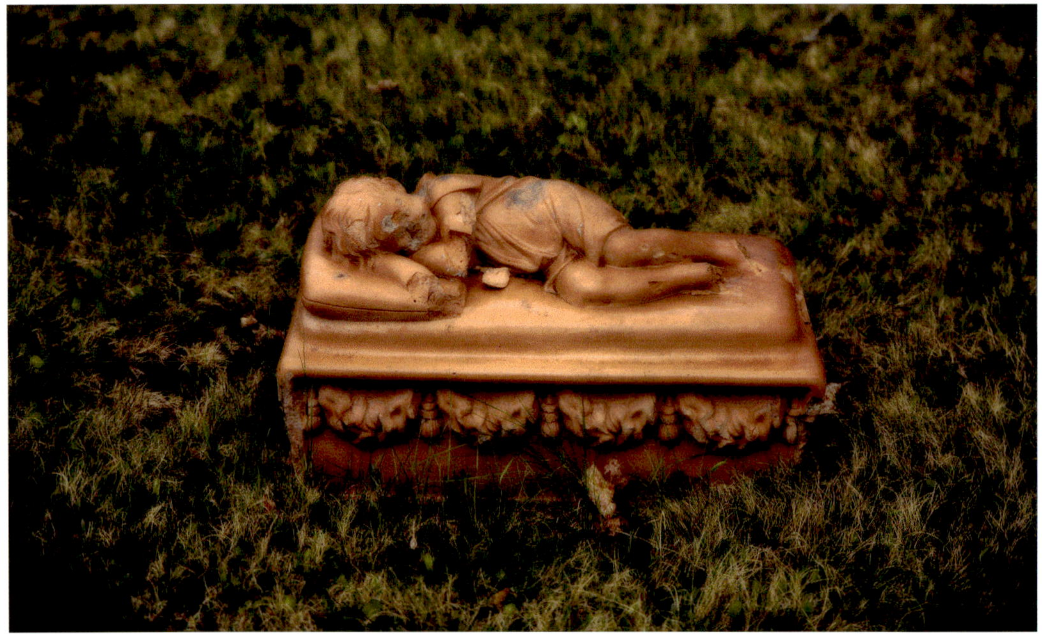

This statue of a child sleeping on a casket indicates an infant or stillborn child has been buried in this location at a family burial plot.

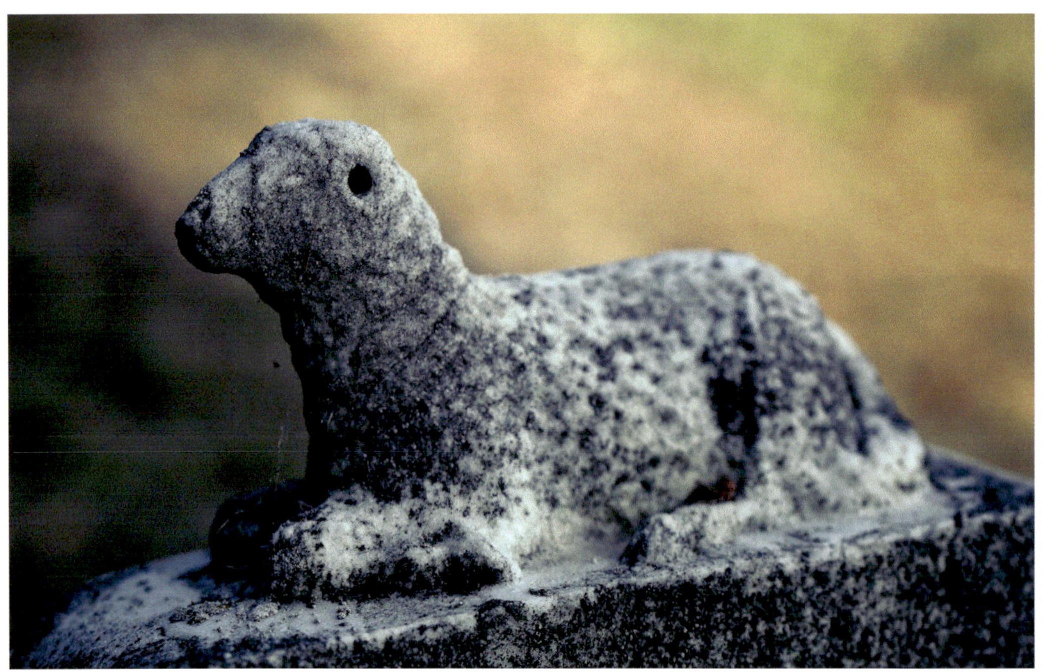

Often if the child is stillborn and was never given a name, a simple block of granite with a lamb figurine on top of it is used to mark the burial site.

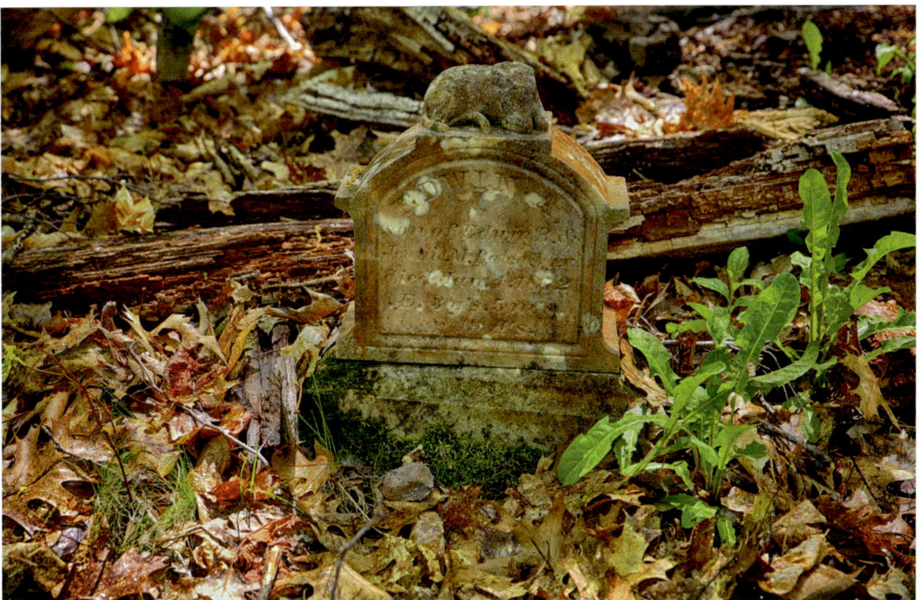

This stone was set apart on the outer edge of the cemetery, grown-in and covered over. It marks the spot of interment for three-year-old Edwin A. Batchelder, son of Edwin B. and Jennie M.; he died on January 4, 1872.

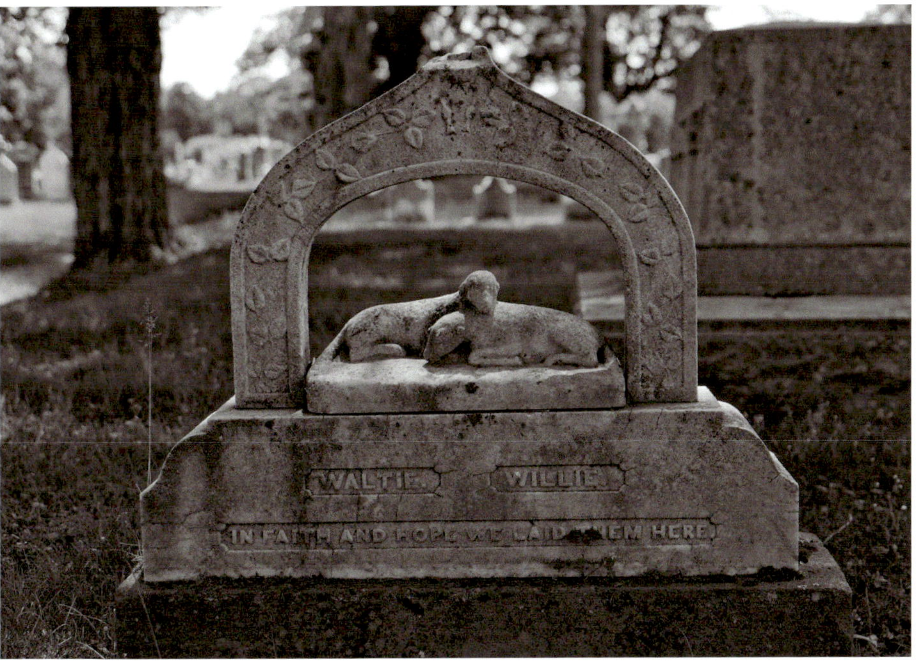

I encountered many lamb statues and angel figurines that represent the graves of lost children, but this was one of the most unique that I have seen. Oak Grove Cemetery, Gardiner.

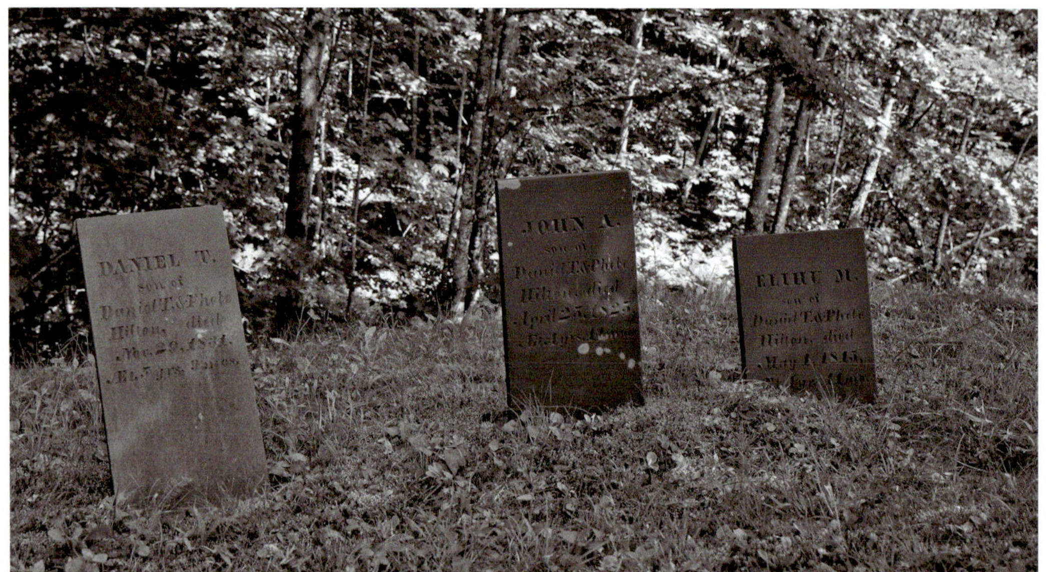

Daniel and Phebe Hilton lost three sons over the course of sixteen years. Elihu M. died on May 1, 1815, at twenty-three months old. On April 25, 1825, the couple lost their son John A. who was four years old. Six years later on November 29, 1831, the couple's third son, Daniel T. died; he was five years old.

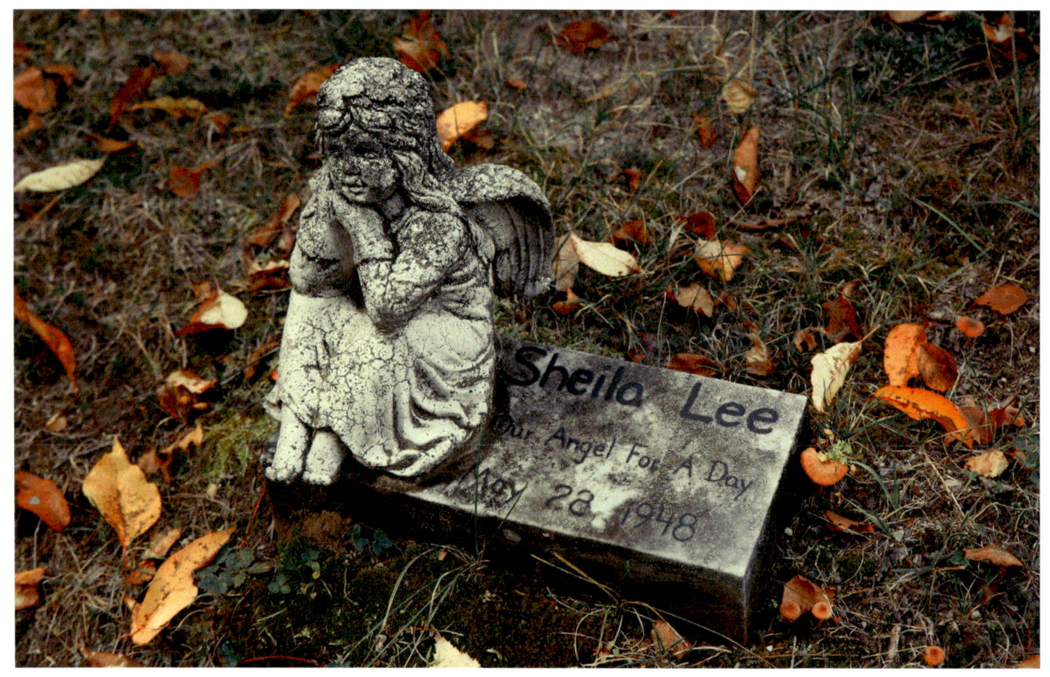

No other information is available for Sheila Lee who lived for but a day in central Maine on May 28, 1948.

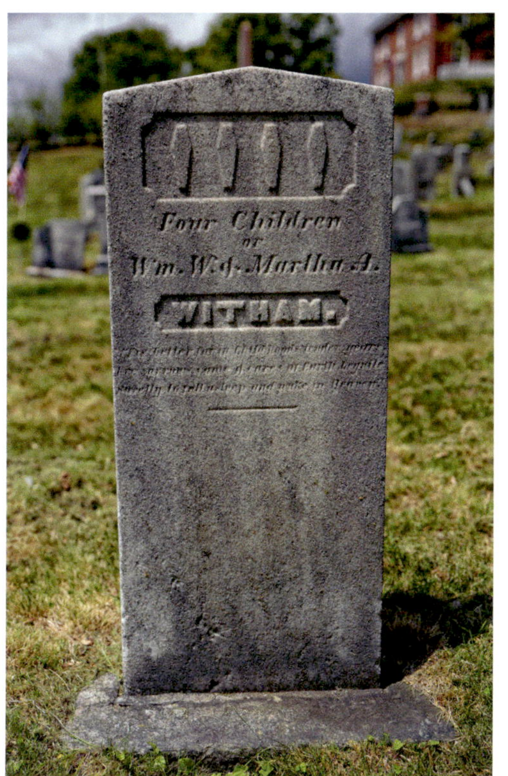

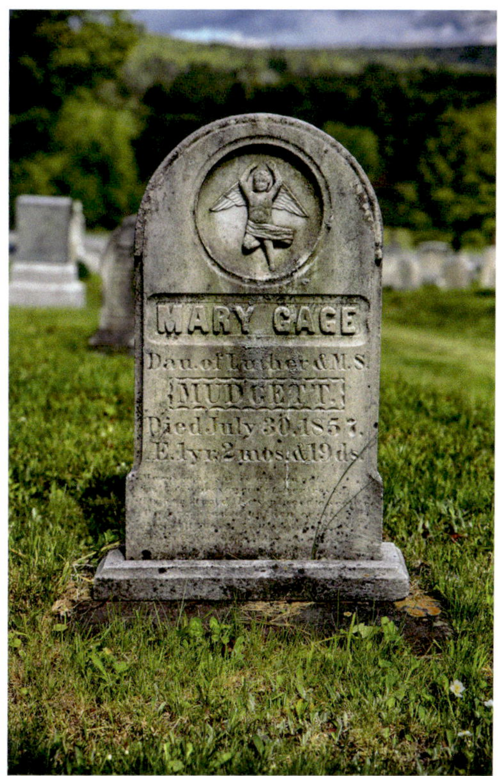

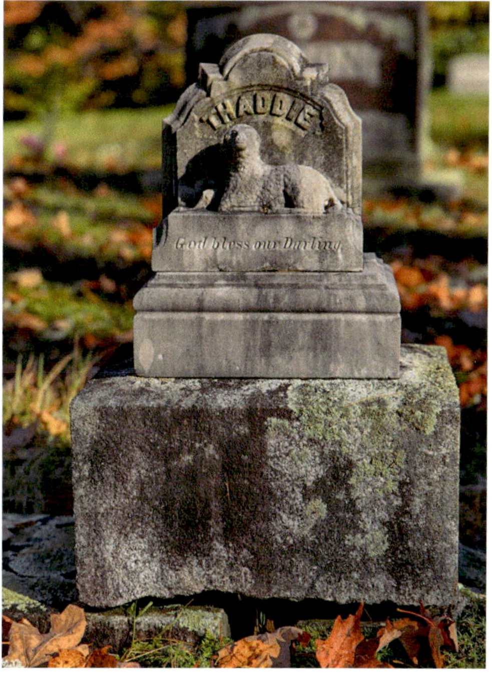

Above left: This is the gravestone of the four children of Mr. and Mrs. Witham. Unfortunately, there are no dates on the stone, and even though there is an epitaph, the letters are worn down rendering the words illegible.

Above right: Fourteen-month-old Mary Gage Mudgett died on July 30, 1857. Only the first line of her epitaph can be read, "Mary's gone, she is an angel."

Right: The lamb marker of young Thaddie with the inscription "God bless our Darling."

63

11

Unique Stones and Unusual Endings

The images in this chapter contain stones that I found unique or unusual, including the manner in which some of the departed left us.

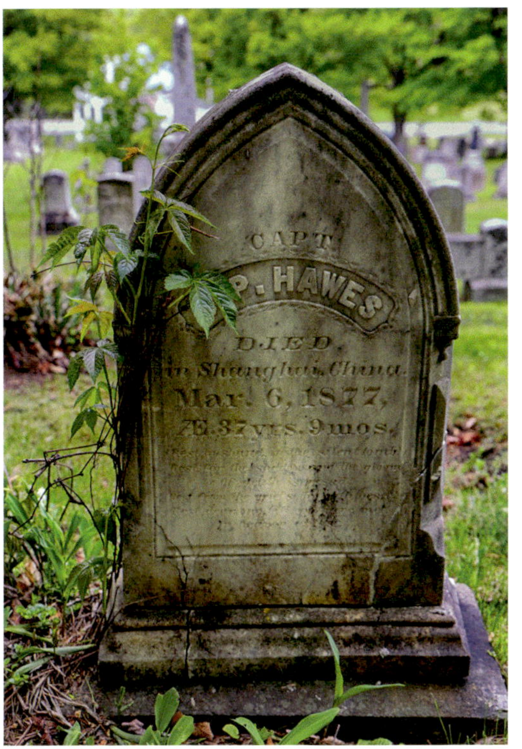

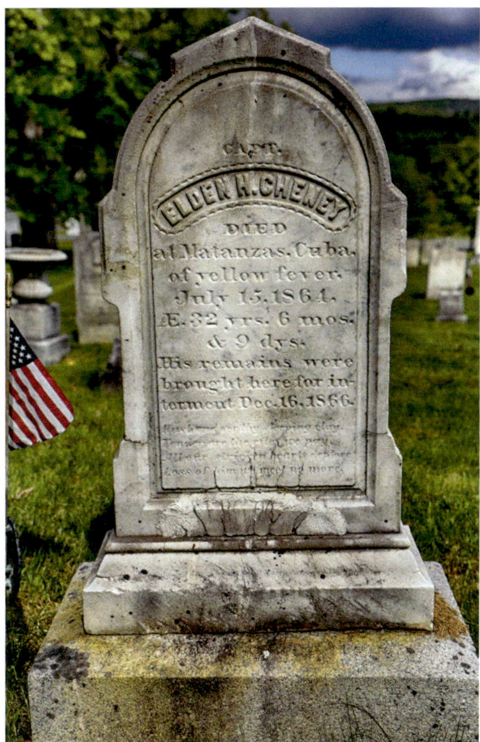

Above left: Captain Hawes died in Shanghai, China on March 6, 1877; he was thirty-seven years old. Perhaps it is just my vivid imagination, but I can conjure up many scenarios as to how a captain might meet his demise in Shanghai, China, during the 1800s.

Above right: Captain Cheney died of yellow fever while he was in Cuba. He was thirty-two years old, and it took a little more than two years for his remains to be brought home to Maine.

Right: Jonathan and Mary Barrell outlived four sons, Octavius, Oliver, George, and Joseph. All of them died while away in various parts of the United States, or in the case of George, on a steamship.

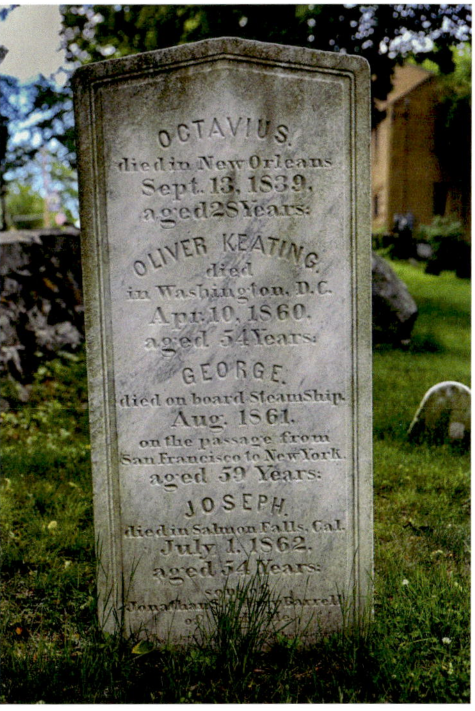

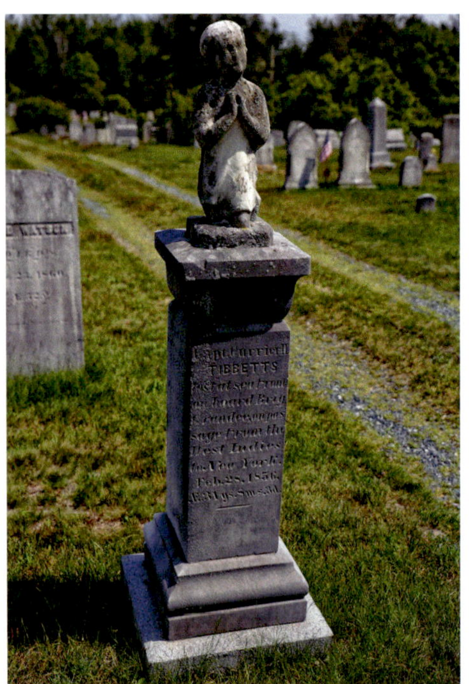

Left: Captain Currier Tibbetts was lost at sea on board the brig *Grandee* during passage from the West Indies to New York, February 28, 1856; he was thirty-one years old.

Below left: This stone was leaning forward, protecting it from the elements and it was in remarkable condition. It is the stone of Mary E., the adopted daughter of Warren and Willmot Huntley who died on May 28, 1852, at the age of eighteen. The stone is simply inscribed: "Mary hath chosen that good part."

Below right: This Angel of Grief monument was erected by Mary E. Chase-Brooks in memory of her departed husband, Dr. John George Brooks, who was a physician and prominent community leader in Belfast before his death in 1904. His grieving widow imported the hand-sculpted angel from Italy in 1905.

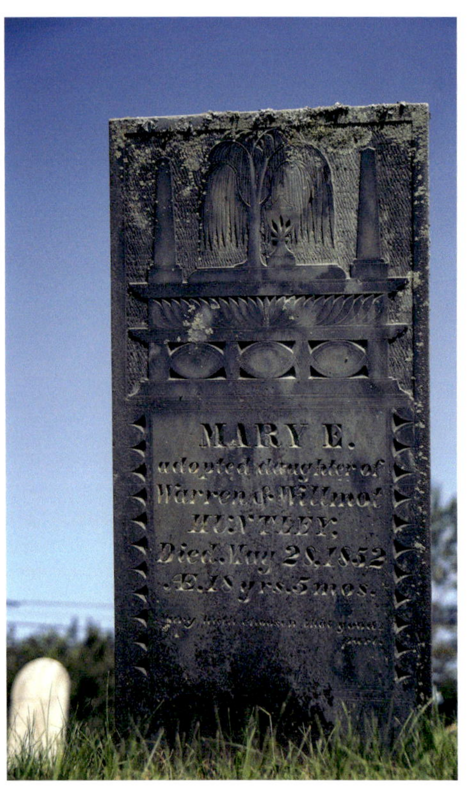

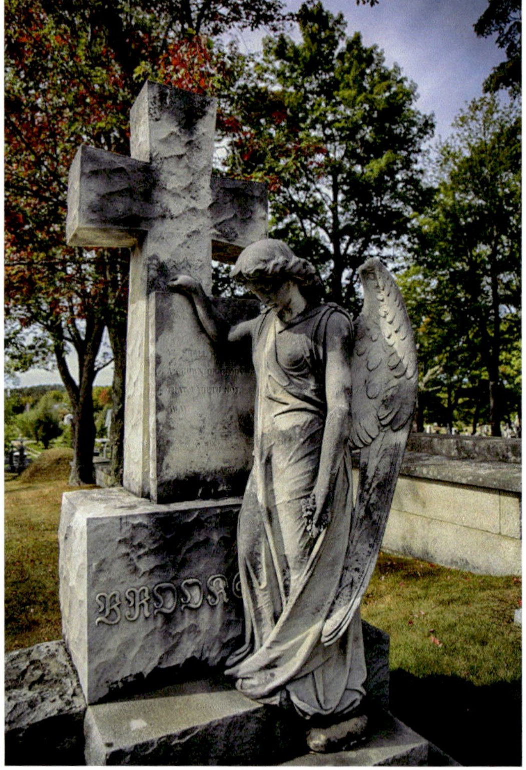

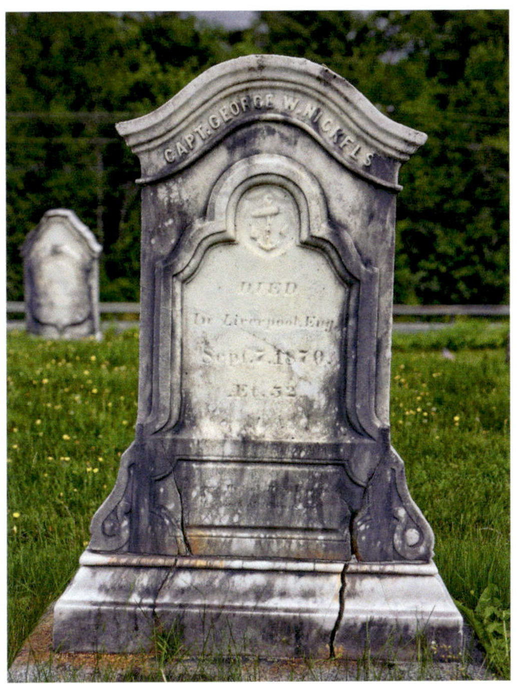

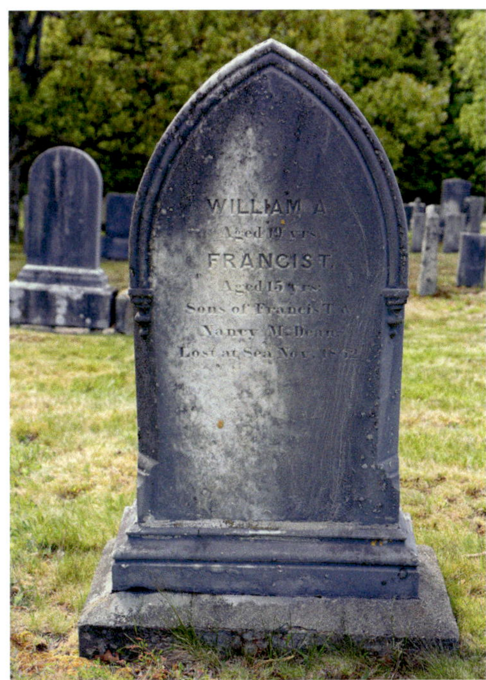

Above left: Captain George W. Nickels died in Liverpool, England, on September 7, 1870; he was fifty-two years old. Maine has many coastal communities along its more than 3,000 miles of tidal coastline, so it stands to reason that many captains are buried in cemeteries along the coast. The stones of captains are always quite unique, not unlike the captains themselves who dedicated their entire lives to the sea.

Above right: William Cain was nineteen years old when he and his brother, fifteen-year-old Francis, Jr., were lost at sea. The grieving parents were Nancy and Francis Dean.

Right: Nancy M., wife of Captain Daniel Blake, died while on passage from New Orleans to New York on March 1, 1858. Her location was latitude 28.44N, longitude 88.52W. I am unable to discern the entire poem on the bottom of the stone, but the first verse is inscribed, "Billows cease thy wild commotion/Death is on an errand here/One is taken for promotion/ to a higher holier sphere." Nancy was twenty-four years old.

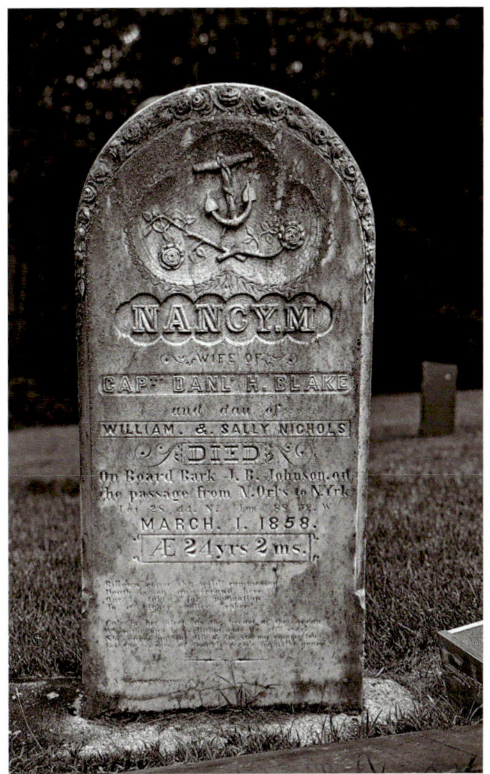

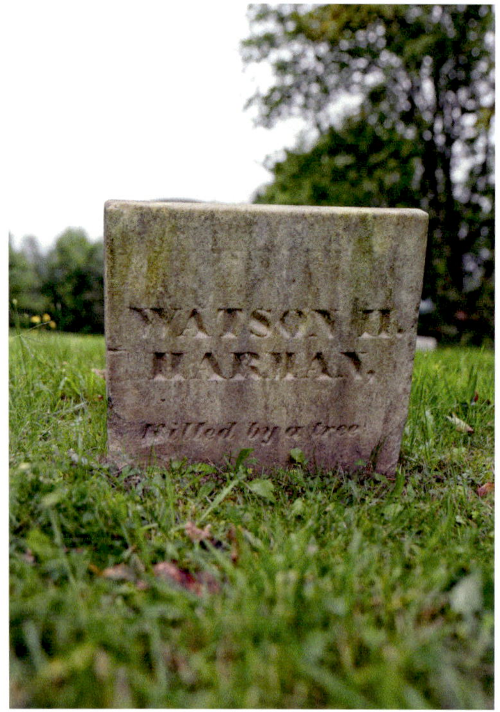

Left: Harman Watson II was killed by a tree. I am not sure what more I can say, and apparently, no one else had much more to say either.

Below left: Fifteen-year-old James Alexander died in December 1786. This unique headstone is in remarkable shape considering it is 238 years old.

Below right: The Oak Grove Cemetery in Bath covers about 40 acres of land and currently has more than fourteen-thousand interments. Mary Sewall was the very first. She died on January 22, 1777; she was thirty-four years old.

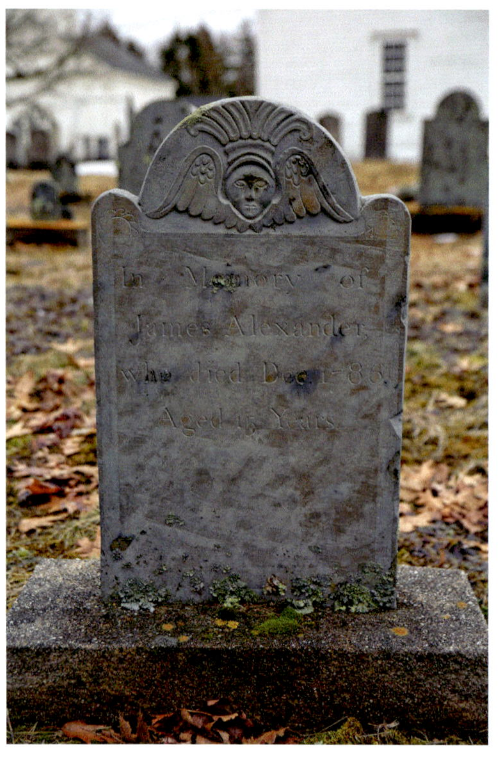

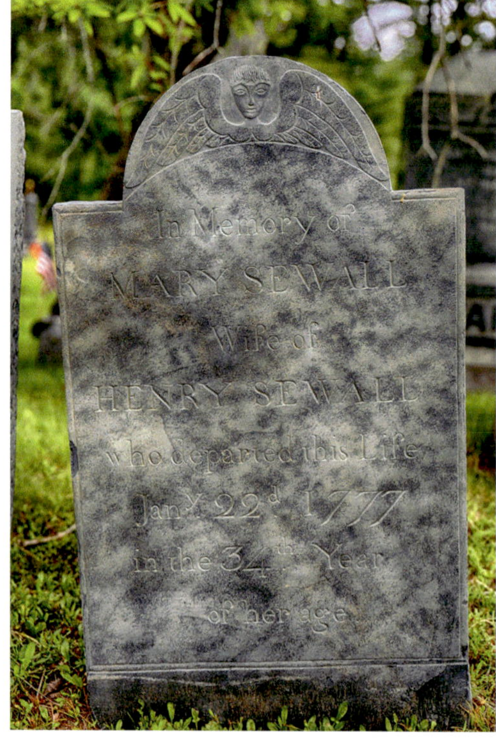

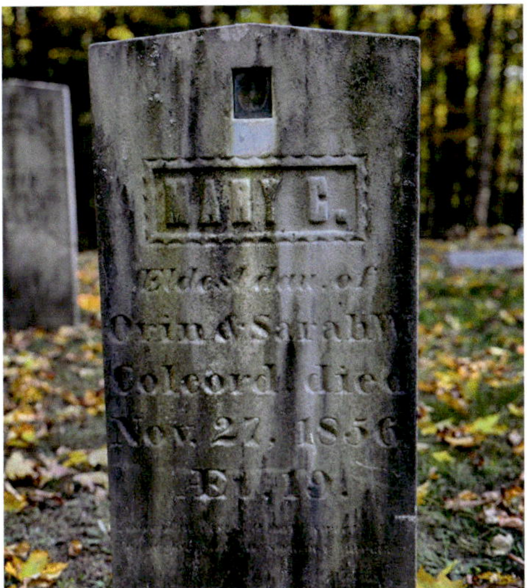

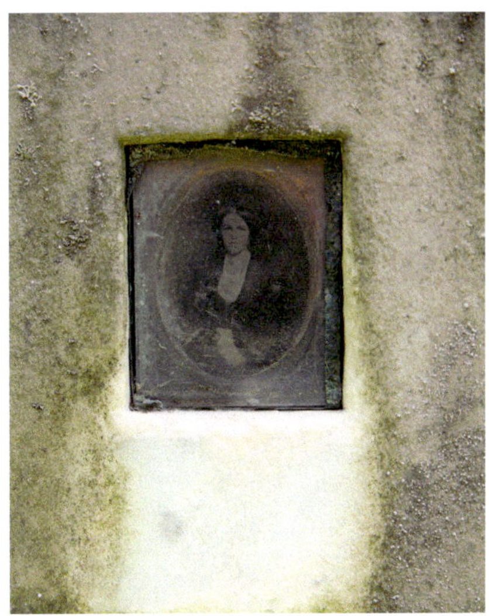

Above left: As I mentioned earlier in this book, there was a brief period in the mid-nineteenth century when portraits were inserted into some gravestones. Unfortunately, this is the only one I have found to be intact. Many are just empty slots, and others show evidence that the portrait has deteriorated.

Above right: Mary Colcord died on November 27, 1856; she was a beautiful nineteen-year-old woman, and I know this because of the portrait on her headstone.

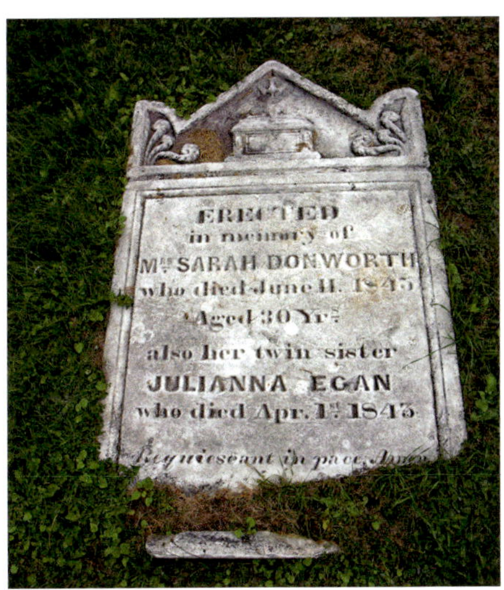

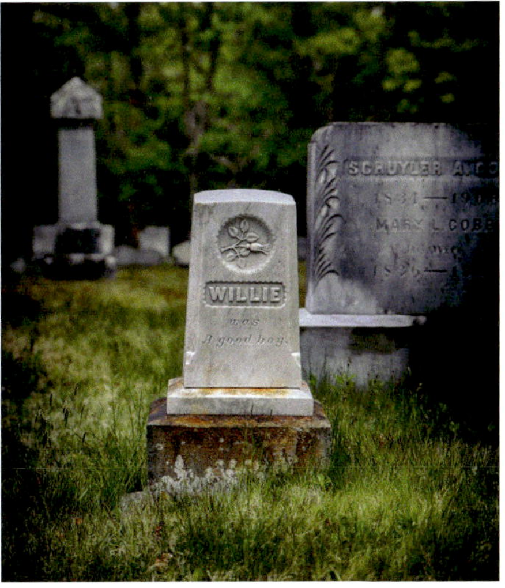

Above left: Sarah and Julianna were twin sisters who both lived to be thirty years old before they died the same year within three months of one another.

Above right: Not all the loss that we grieve is because we lose a human companion. Many people experience profound loss when losing a pet, not unlike losing a child, or a loved human partner.

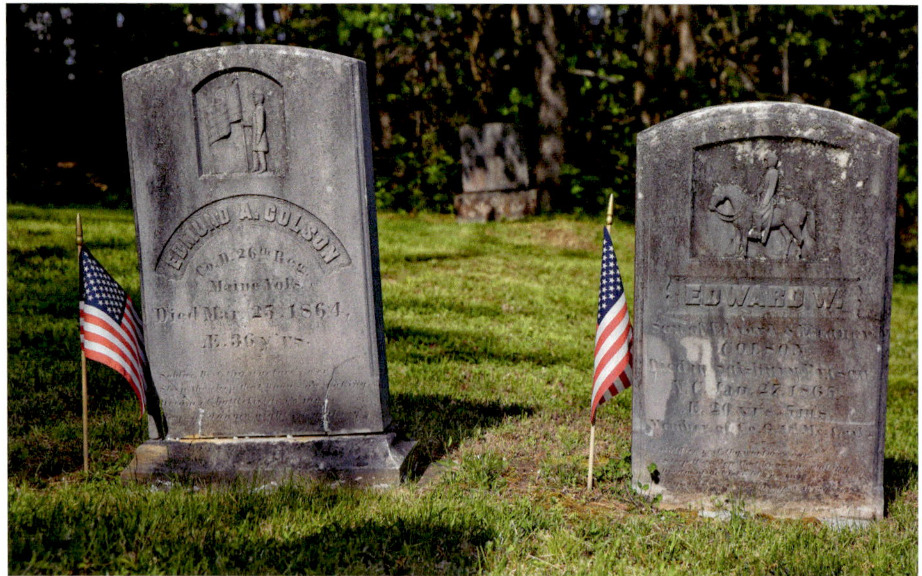

Brothers in Arms: The Colson brothers both died during the Civil War. Twenty-year-old Edward (right) died a POW in Salisbury Prison, North Carolina, on January 27, 1865. Both stones utilize the poetry of Sir Walter Scott in their epitaphs, "Soldier, rest thy warfare o'er/ Sleep the sleep that knows not breaking/ Dream of battled fields no more/ Days of Danger, nights of waking."

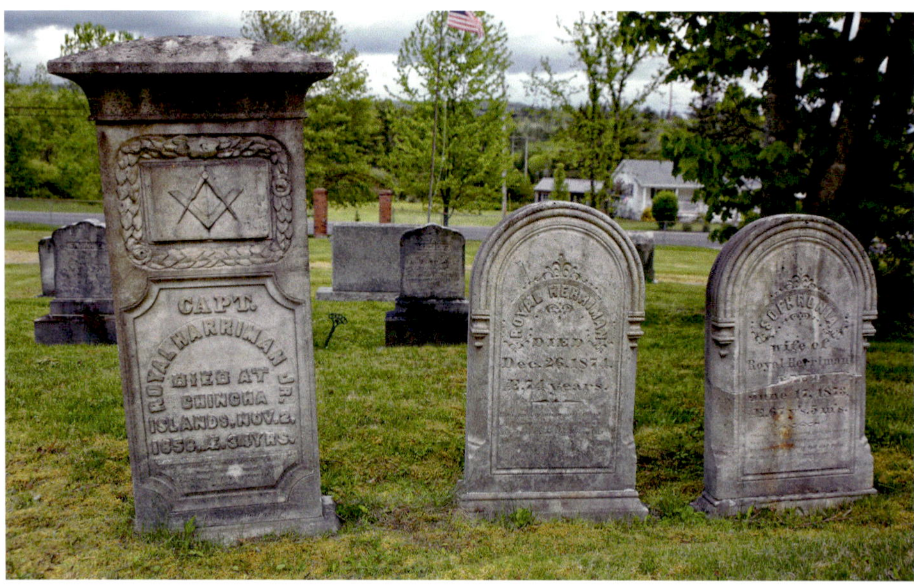

Captain Royal Harriman, Jr., (far left) died at the Chincha Islands on November 2, 1858; he was thirty-four years old. He is buried beside his parents, Royal and Sophronia Harriman, and the following epitaph is on his stone: "Thy memory shall never fade from our hearts until the last leaf of the acacia shall wither."

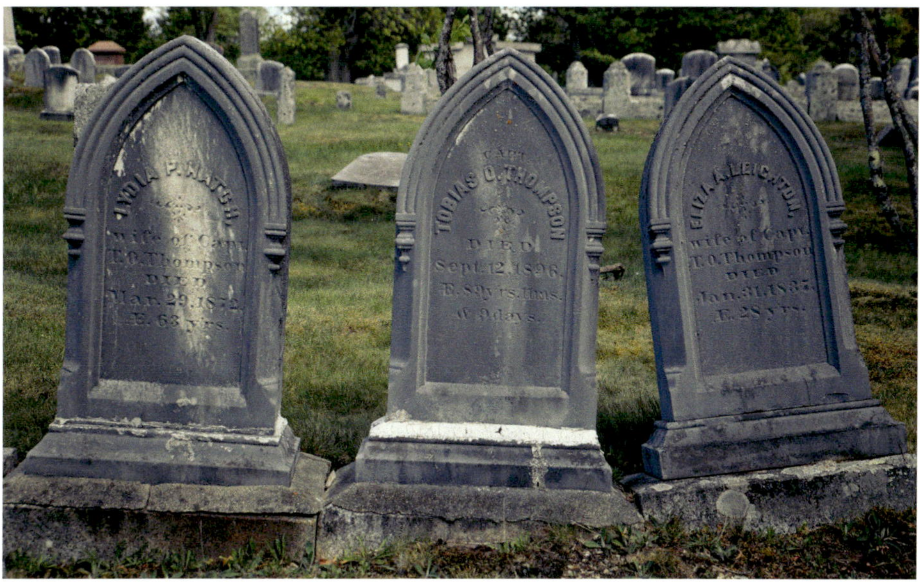

Captain Tobias Thompson stayed true to his first wife as well as his second. Poor Eliza died in 1837 at the age of twenty-eight. Captain Thompson's second wife, Lydia, died in 1872 at the age of sixty-three.

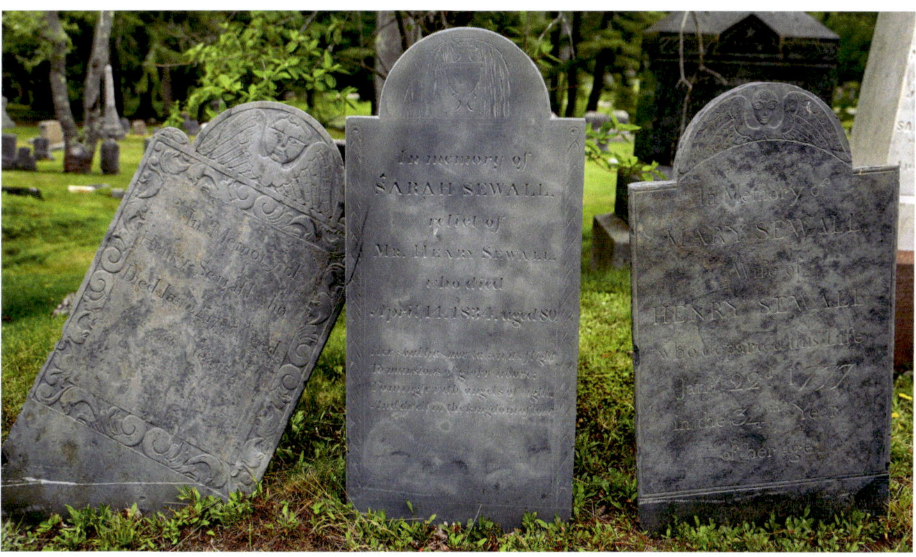

It is interesting to see the stages that gravestones have gone through regarding their design and type. For instance, these three stones are all slate, but we can see from the earliest stone on the right (mentioned earlier, lower right image on p. 68), the stone was simply carved with nothing elaborate. The stone on the far left is from 1795, nearly twenty years later, and we can see much more elaborate detail on the carving with the introduction of scrollwork on the edges. The most recent stone in the middle (Sarah Sewall, 1834) shows that the death's head has gone out of favor which occurred at the turn of the century when it was replaced by the urn and willow tree.

12

Everlasting Epitaphs

Since the advent of the written word, we have used the poetry and prose of epitaphs to express ourselves and convey our feelings in a way that others can understand and appreciate them. The epitaph is arguably the most poignant of all our forms of expression because it allows us to share lamentations over our dead or it allows us to share one final message as we depart this plane of existence.

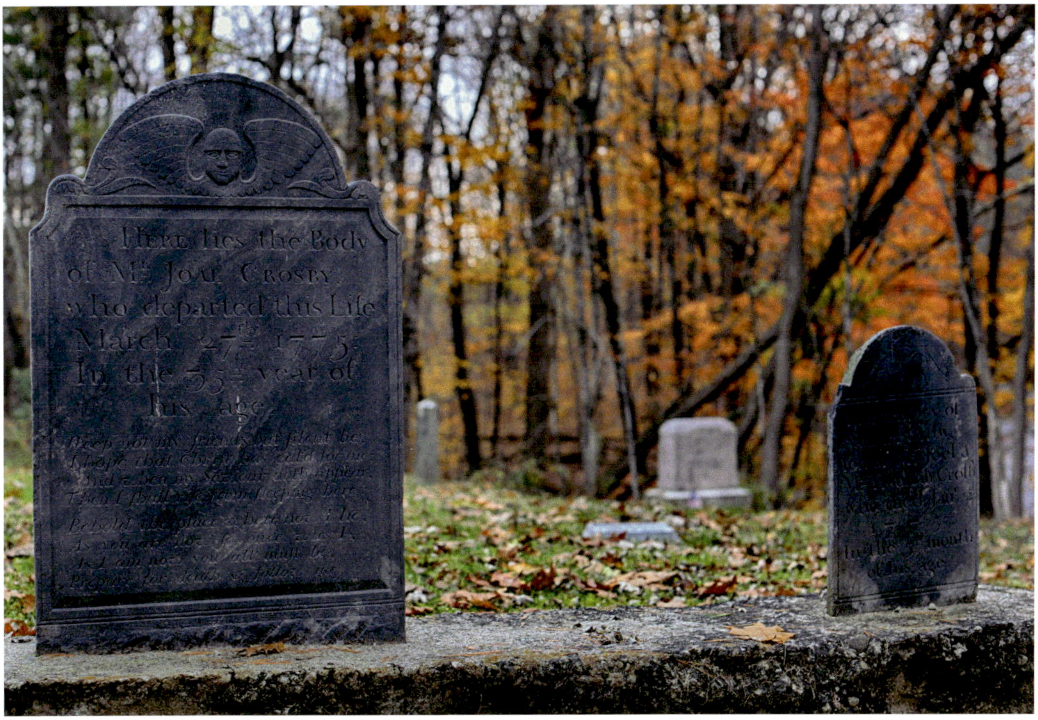

Above: Joal Crosby, March 27, 1775. "Weep not my friends but silent be/ I hope that Christ has cal'd for me/ And when my Savior doth appear/ then I shall rise from sleeping here/ Behold the place where I now lie/ As you are now so once was I/ As I am now you all must be/ Prepare for death & follow me."

Right: "Here lies the body of Richard Thomas/ An inglishman by birth/ A whig of 76/ By occupation a Cooper/ Now food for worms/ Like an old rumpuncheon marked number and shooked/ He will be raised again and finished by his creator/ He died Sep. 28, 1824, aged 75/ America my adopted country/ My best advice to you is to take care of your liberties."

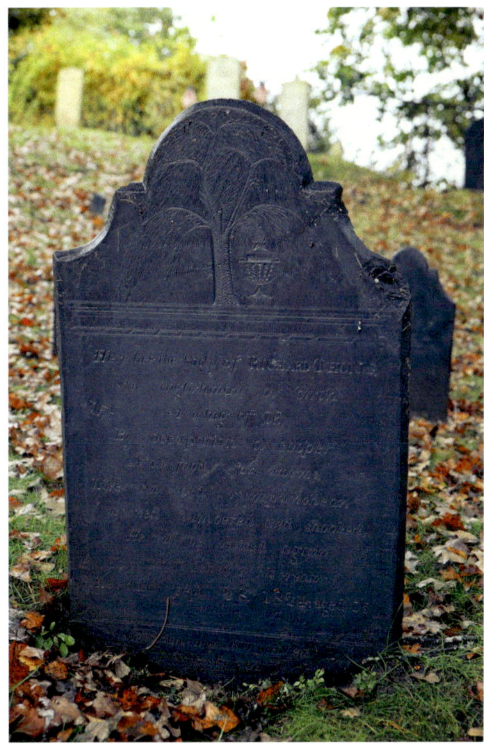

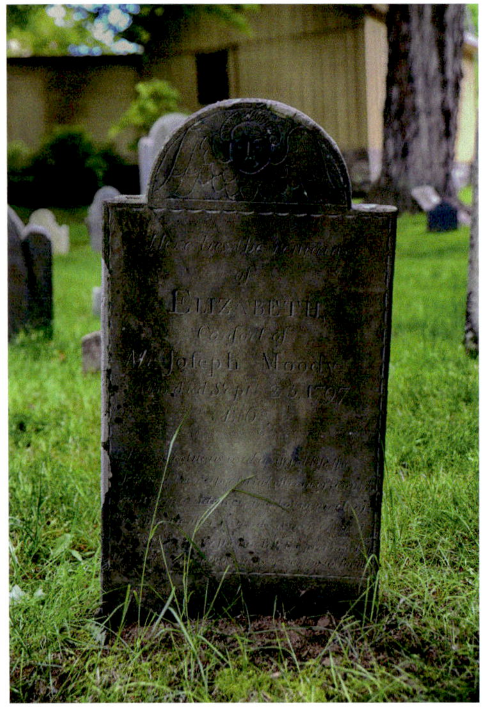

Left: Elizabeth Moody, September 23, 1797. "By a virtuous and useful life she secured the respect and esteems of a numerous acquaintance, and to the circle of her particular friends, who were witness of her piety, she has left the precious ho'p that she is now in possession of ye reward of the faithful."

Below left: Delmont Genn died on May 31, 1848, at the age of thirty-three. "Rest, loved one, rest, thy sorrows now are o'er/ And pain and sicknes, thou shalt know no more/ Rest, till the God who gave thee to decay/ Shall rise thee to the realms of endless day."

Below right: Rosie Killman left this earth on October 29, 1880; she was twenty-one years old. "O for the touch of a vanished hand/ And the sound of a voice that is still."

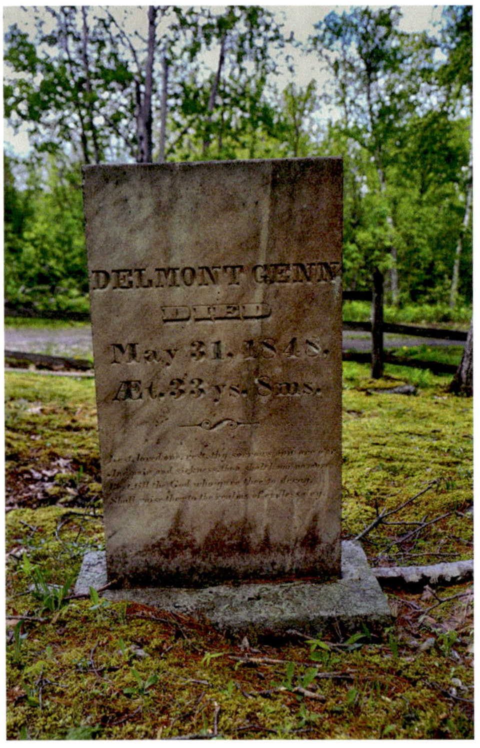

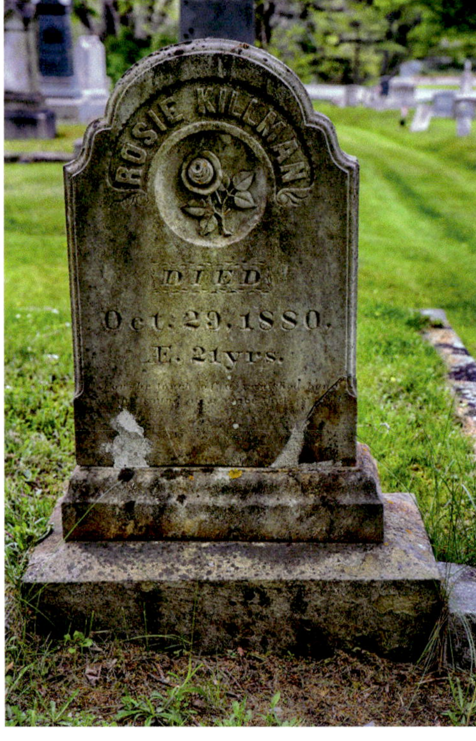

Right: Mary Jane, wife of Captain Andrew Grant, died on March 24, 1853, age twenty-three. "Calm be thy sleep as the breast of the ocean/ When the sun is reclining upon its still wave/ She dreams not of life or its stormy commotion/ For the surges of trouble recede from the grave."

Below left: Jotham Sewall, October 2, 1854, twenty-seven years old. "One we love has left our number/ For the dark and silent tomb/ Closed his eyes in breathless slumber/ Faded in his early bloom/ But long his memory will be revered/ By those who knew his worth/ By those whom he was endeared/ By strongest ties of earth."

Below right: Sarah Thomas' stone was only partly legible. Here are two stanzas of her lovely epitaph: "The grave cannot hide thee still lovely and fair/ thy soft image floats with bright spirits of air/ As the halo of love that thy life did illum-/ Soft memories shall cluster in wreaths o'er thy tomb."

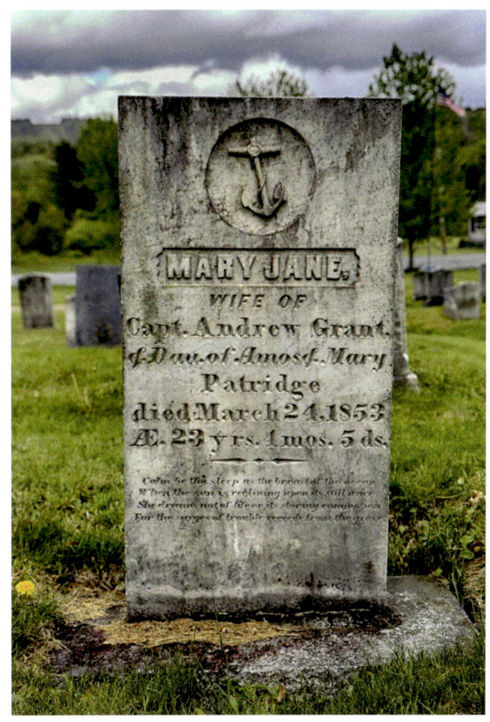

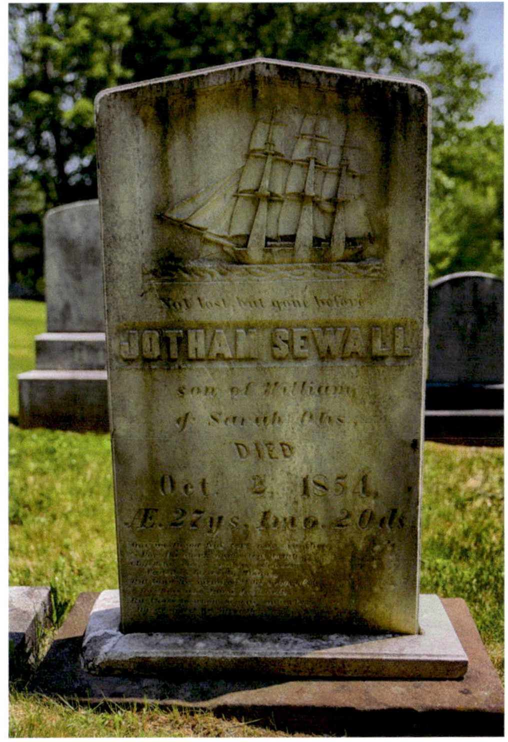

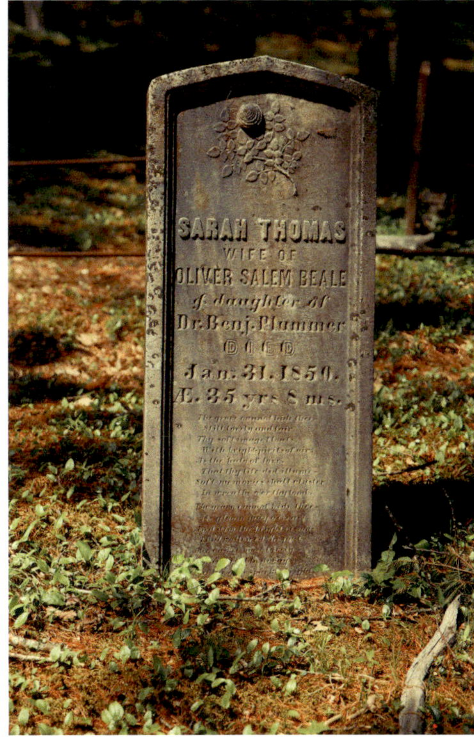

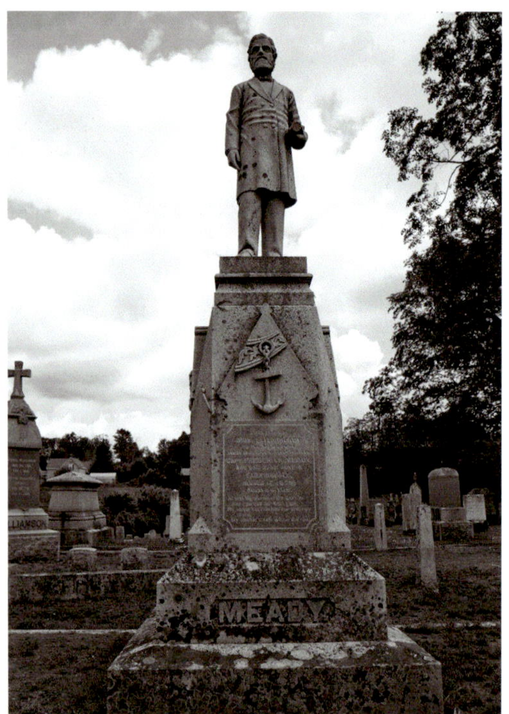

Left: Captain Frederick Meady, 1823–1879: "At last the storms of life are over and I survive the final gale/ My barque has reached the heavenly shore/ My anchor's safe within the veil."

Below left: I was fortunate to discover this stone before it was entirely swallowed up by the earth. Laura M. Sperry was buried here on June 22, 1856. Her epitaph reads, "Lone are the paths, and sad the hours/ When thy sweet smile is gone/ But O, a brighter home than ours/ In heaven is now thine own."

Below right: Eliza Ann Blanchard's inscription utilizes the first stanza of the poem "So fades the lovely, blooming flower" by Anne Steele, 1760. "So fades the lovely, blooming flower/ Frail, smiling solace of an hour/ So soon our transient comforts fly/ And pleasure only blooms to Die!"

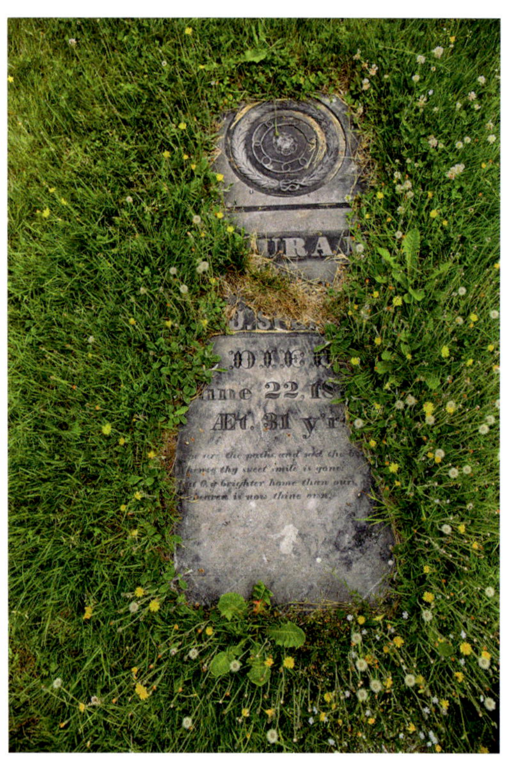

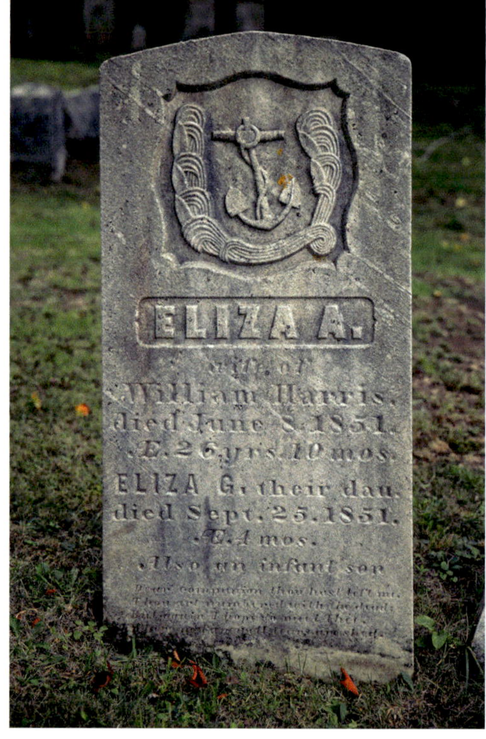

Right: The atheist's grave: "I came without my own consent/liv'd a few years much discontent/ At human errors grieving/ I rul'd myself by reasons laws/But got contempt and not applause/ Because of disbelieving/ For nothing e'er could me convert/ To faith some people did assert/ Alone would gain salvation/ But now the grave does me inclose/ The superstitious will suppose/ I'm doomed to Hell's damnation/ But as to that they do not know/ Opinions oft from ignorance flow/ Devoid of sure foundation/ T is easy men should be deceiv'd/ When any thing by them's believ'd/ Without a demonstration."

Below left: David Trask died during the Civil War in Thibodeaux, Louisianna. "He was a patriot firm and brave/He fought his country's flag to save/But now it floats above his head/As he lies in his lovely bed."

Below right: Sixteen-year-old Mary passed away on August 22, 1862. "Twas hard dear one to part with thee/ To part to meet on earth no more/ We feel our home can never be/ The happy place it was before."

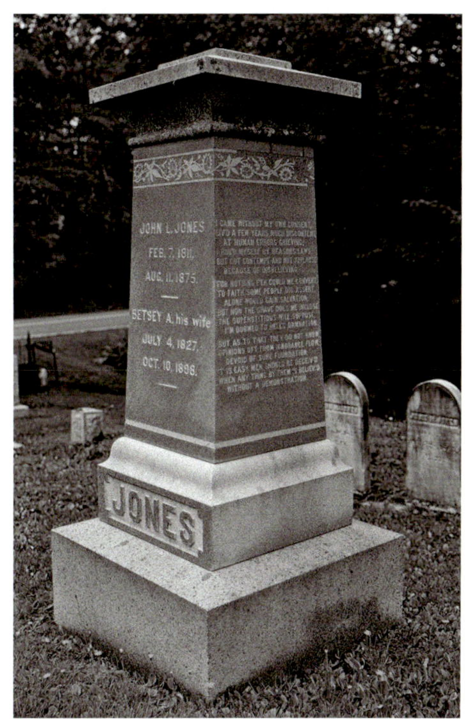

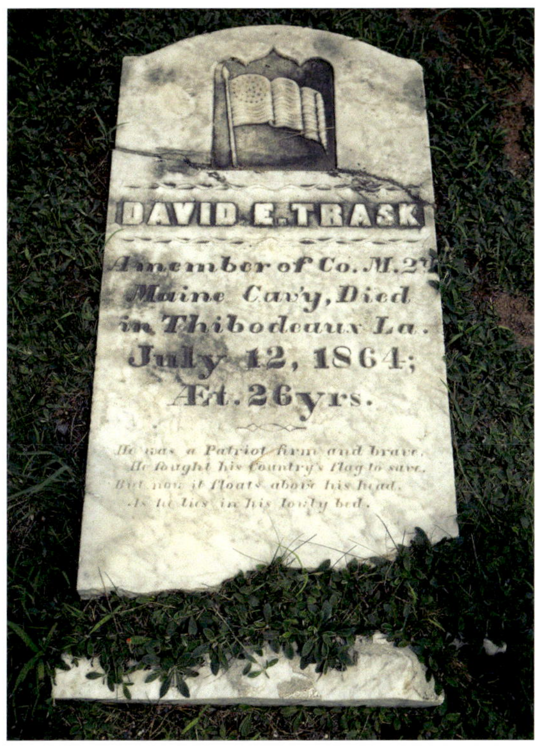

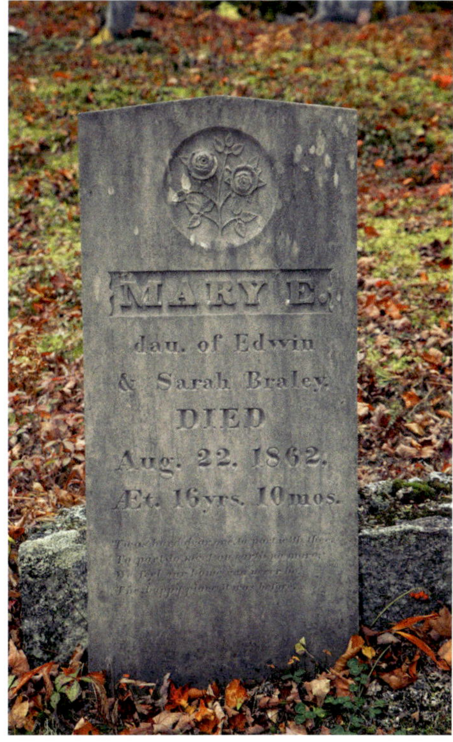

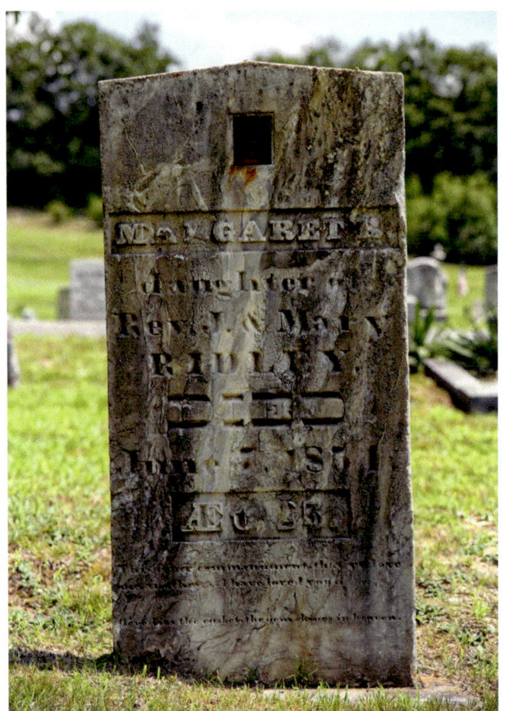

Left: This stone had a tintype portrait at one time which unfortunately has rusted out, leaving only a stain. Most of the stone is quite legible, but some of the inscription is unclear. I have used XXX to indicate missing words. "This is my XXX That ye' love/ me XXX, I have loved you/ Here lies the casket, the gem shines in heaven."

Below left: Clement Skolfield was fifty-six when he died on May 22, 1796. His stone is inscribed with, "The sweet remembrance of the Just/ Shall flourish when they sleep in dust."

Below right: "Weep not for me O husband dear/ I am not dead but sleeping here/ I am not thine but Christ alone/ He loved me best and took me home." Mary Ann Weight to her husband Enoch, November 7, 1856.

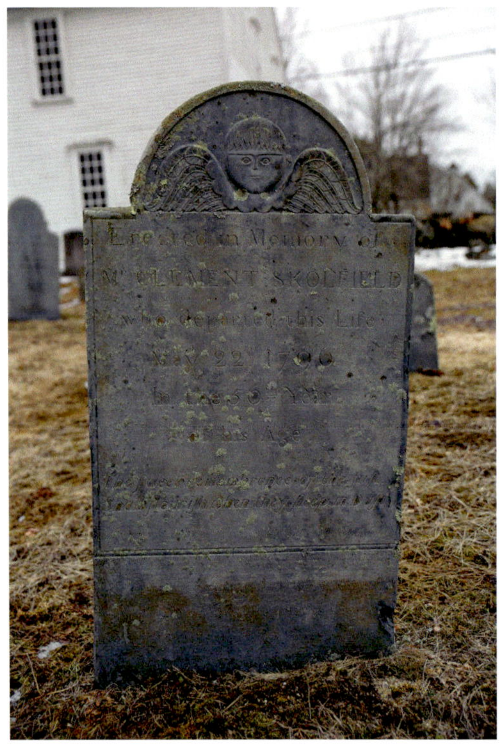

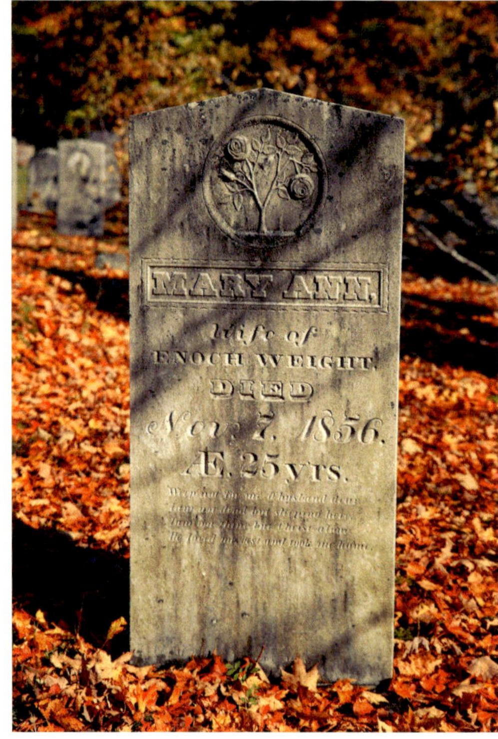

Right: Hiram McAlister was twenty-two years old when he died on November 26, 1851. "He sleeps in Death, his soul has gone/ To those bright realms above/ a beauteous gem by angels borne/ To deck the throne of love/ He's gone, but yet there lingers still/ a thought in memory dear/ and ever will of those blest hours/ of sweet communion here."

Below left: Christania Reynolds was eleven when she passed away on January 14, 1853. Her stone is inscribed with the following epitaph: "Gone like a faded flower/ No more on earth to bloom/ Renewed by Christ redeeming power/ She lives beyond the tomb."

Below right: Margaret Clement died on July 22, 1860; she was twenty-two years old. "She's gone, she's gone, the cherished one/ Her toils are over the victory's won/ Just in the morning of her day/ When hope was bright she pss'd away."

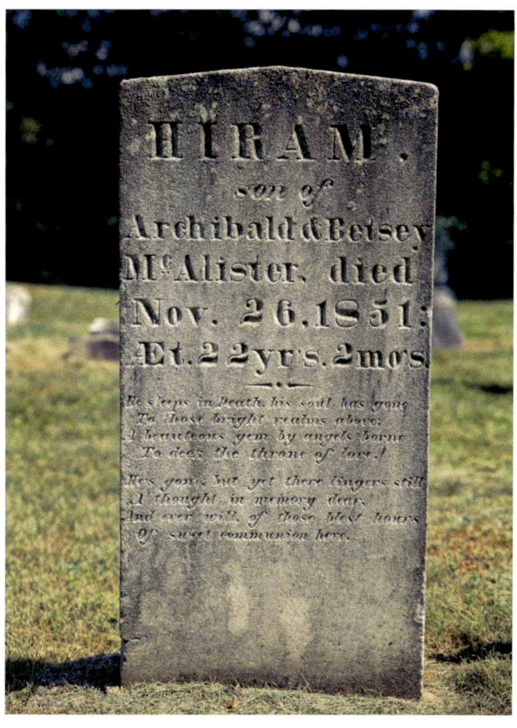

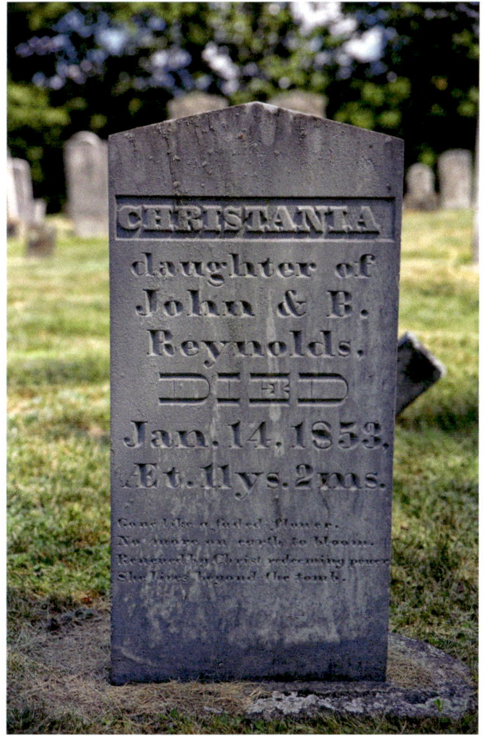

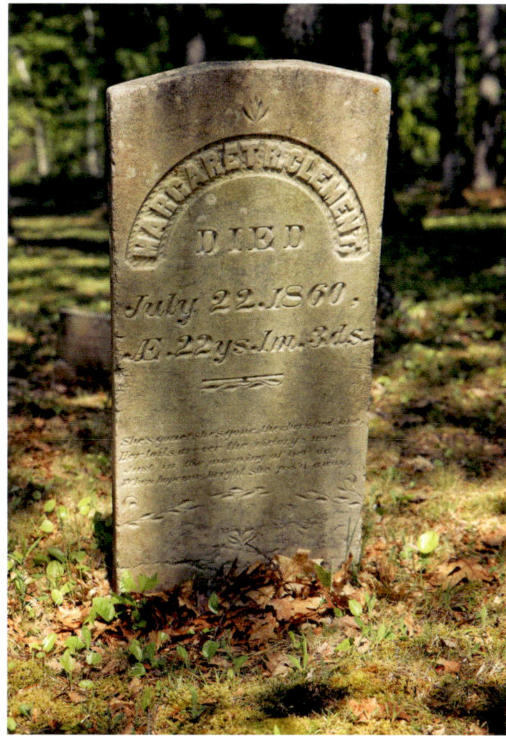

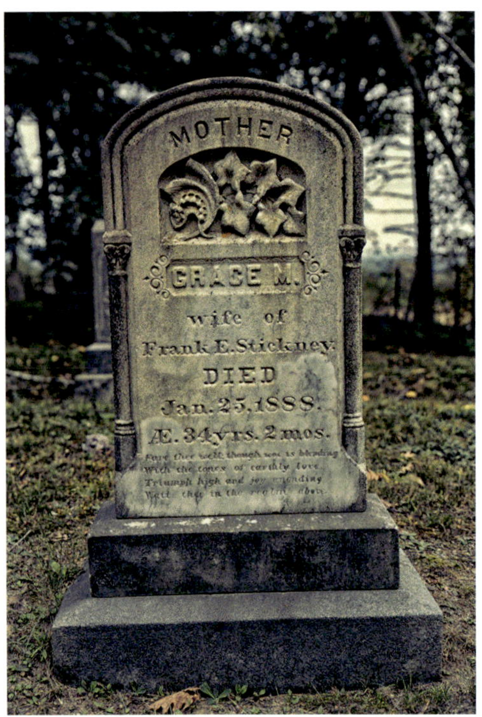

Left: "Fare thee well: though woe is blending/ With the tones of earthly love/ Triumph high and joy unending/ Wait thee in the realm above."

Below left: Thomas Sparhawk Esq., died on June 4, 1807, in his thirty-seventh year. "One eye on death and one full fix'd on Heaven/ Becomes a mortal and immortal man."

Below right: Charles Nelson died in Cardenas on September 6, 1858. The following epitaph is on his stone: "No tears for thou our lone spirits mourn/ that though with spring's sweet flowers will ne'er return/ No tears for the though hearth and home are blighted/ Though sadness clouds the scenes thy love has blighted/ No tears for while with us thy soul oppressed/ Oft longed for refuge in thy Saviors' breast/ No tears for thou hast found thy home above/ No tears thou'rt sheltered in the arms of love."

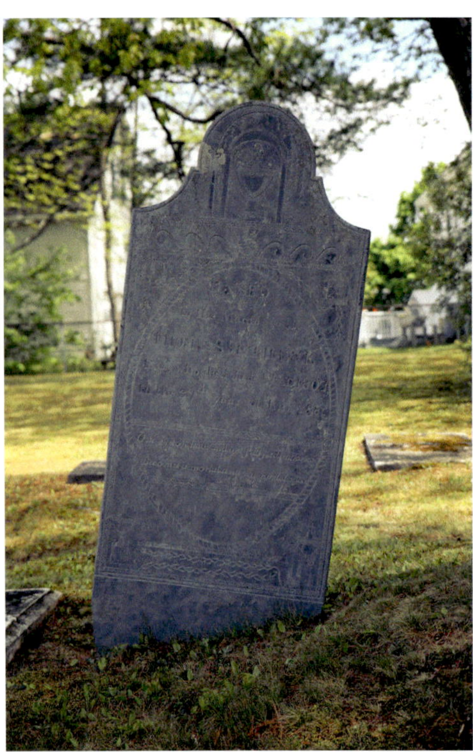

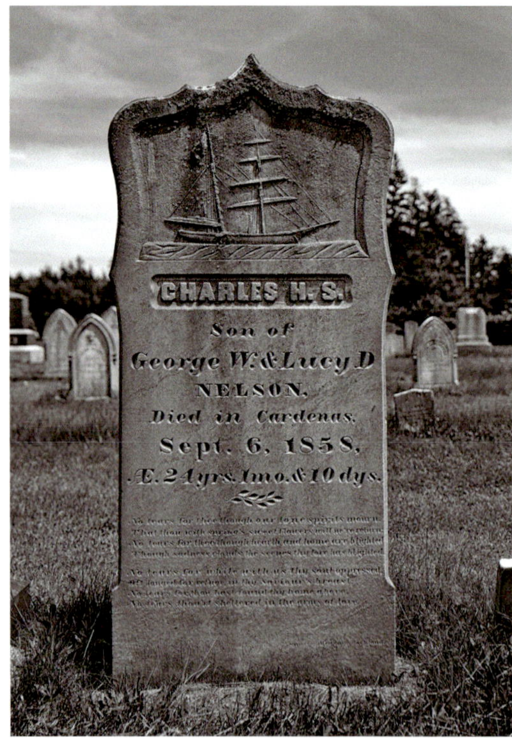

13

Final Resting Places

In the days of the Vikings, the revered dead were packed into a boat with all their belongings and set adrift, only to be ignited by a burning arrow for cremation at sea. In ancient Egypt, an elaborate process of mummification would preserve the body of the deceased rather than have it be subjected to decay.

These extraordinary examples aside, evidence suggests that humankind has been burying its dead since our neanderthal ancestors roamed the earth. Since that time, our species' methods of burial have evolved from simple funerary pits to elaborate burial markers, caskets, and graveside ceremonies.

Over time, our burial sites have gone from unmarked or simply marked graves, to family plots and then large cemeteries. In this chapter, I go around the state and look at cemeteries and burial sites. Breathtaking scenery, unique locations, and special features make Maine cemeteries extremely photogenic, and for the most part, they bring a sense of peace and tranquility to those who visit.

The River Styx, Heaven, Valhalla, or nothingness; we cannot know where those who came before us have gone, or for that matter, where we will go, but here is where the journeys begin.

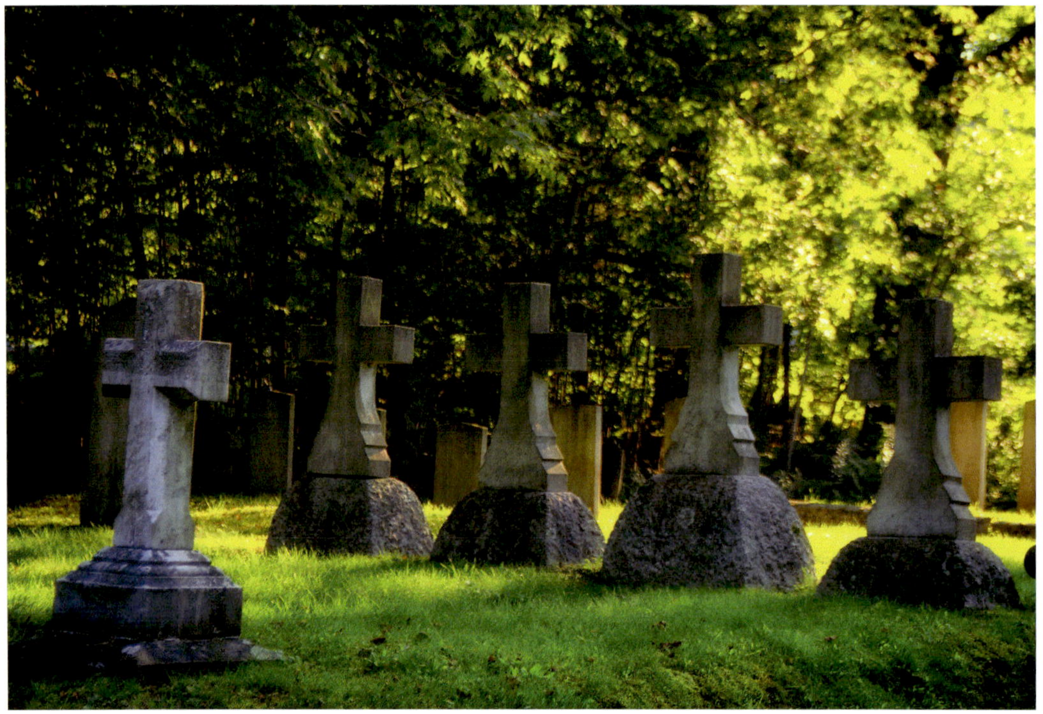

Crosses in the twilight, Mt. Vernon, Maine. Accompanying image for the poem "The Light."

The Light

The Devil may come tomorrow
and cart me off to Hell
but as the sun sets on my days
I do not fear the night

When the darkness comes
before my golden glow is gone
I will follow that which guides
and I will go with the light

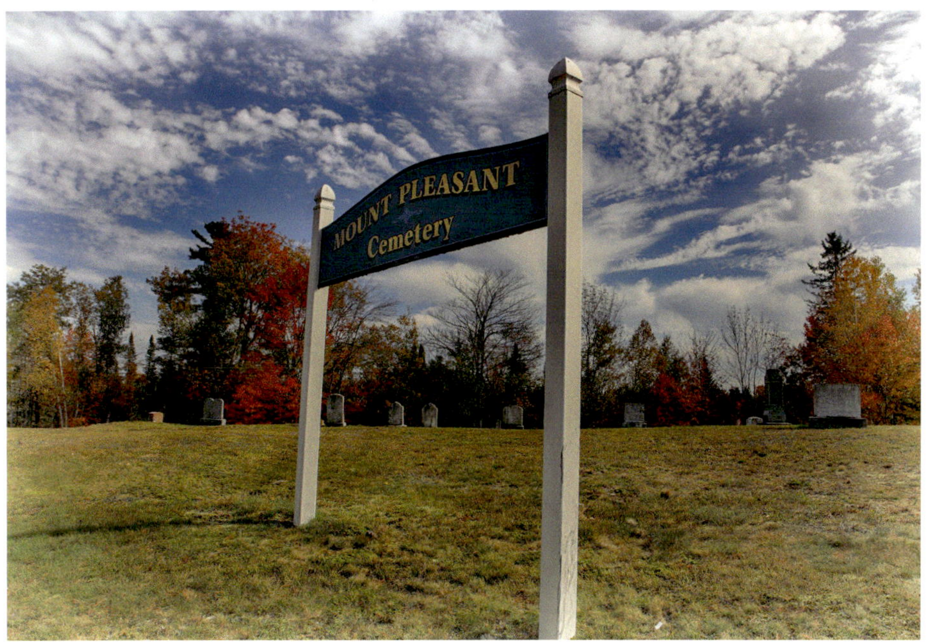

Mount Pleasant Cemetery, Cambridge Maine. This cemetery in Somerset County is still actively being used, its first interment was in 1846.

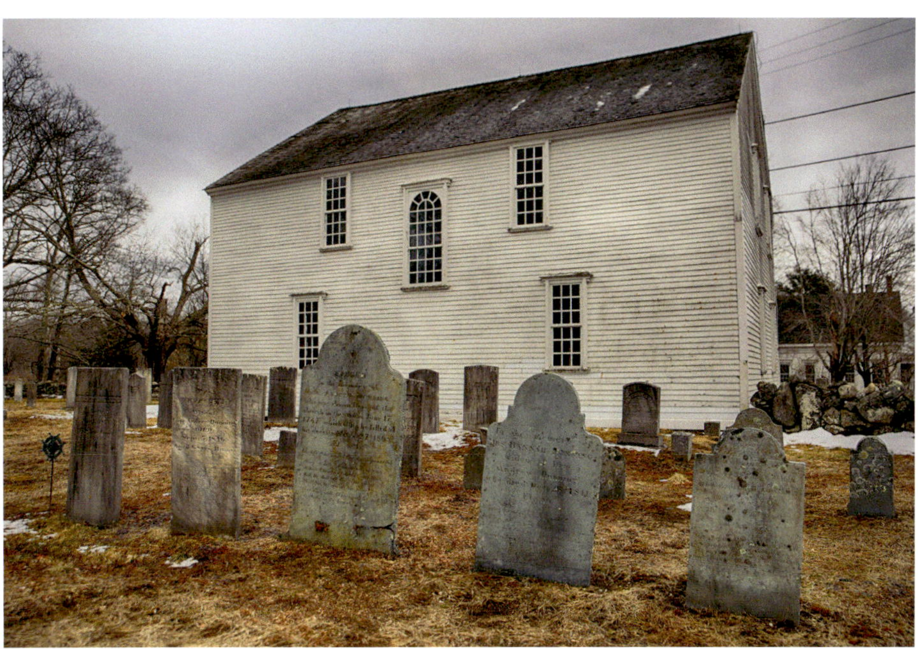

At the Old Harpswell Common Burying Ground in the coastal community of Harpswell, gravestones of early town settlers can be seen with the meetinghouse (*c.* 1757) prominently in the background.

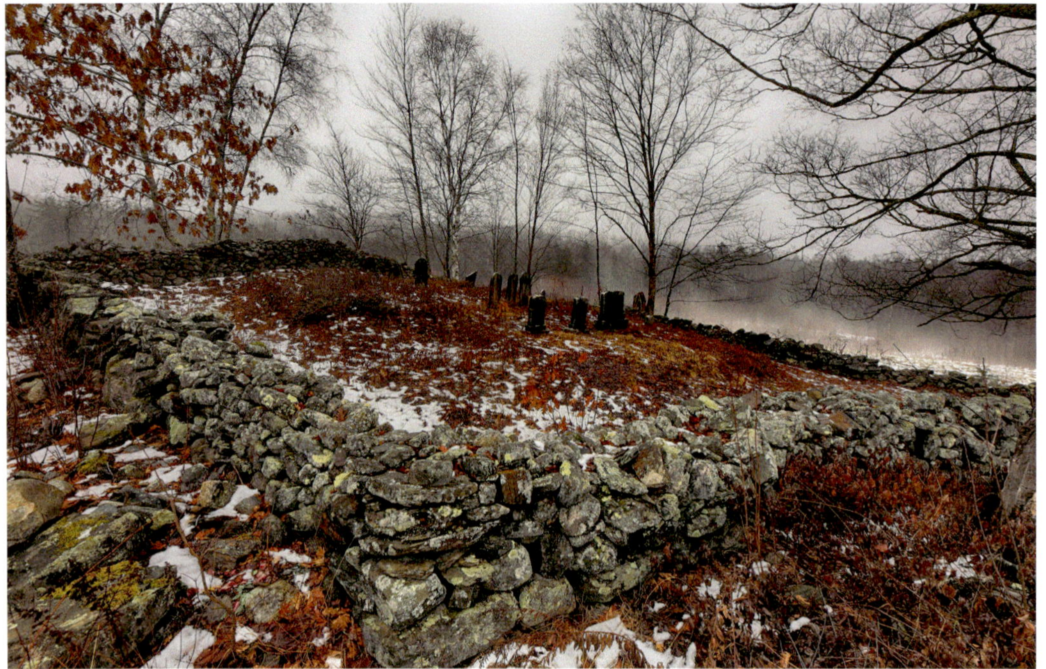

The ground fog creates an ominous, almost surreal scene in this small central Maine cemetery. Stones removed from the nearby farmer's fields were used to create the stonewalls that enclose this graveyard.

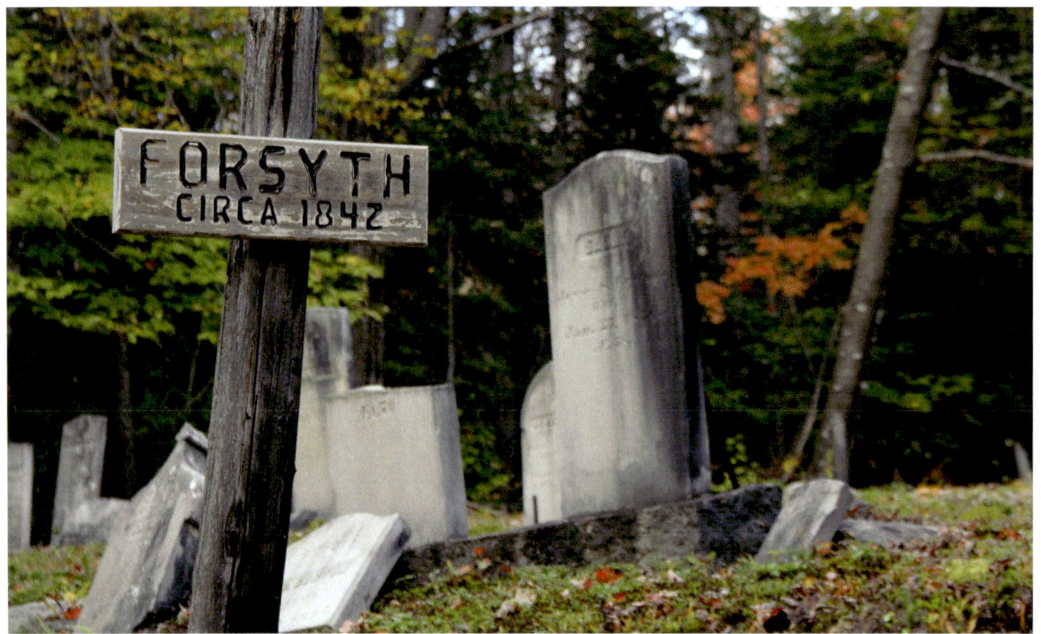

Forsyth Cemetery, St. Albans. The oldest stone on the site is Pricilla Harvey who died in 1842. The cemetery is no longer in use.

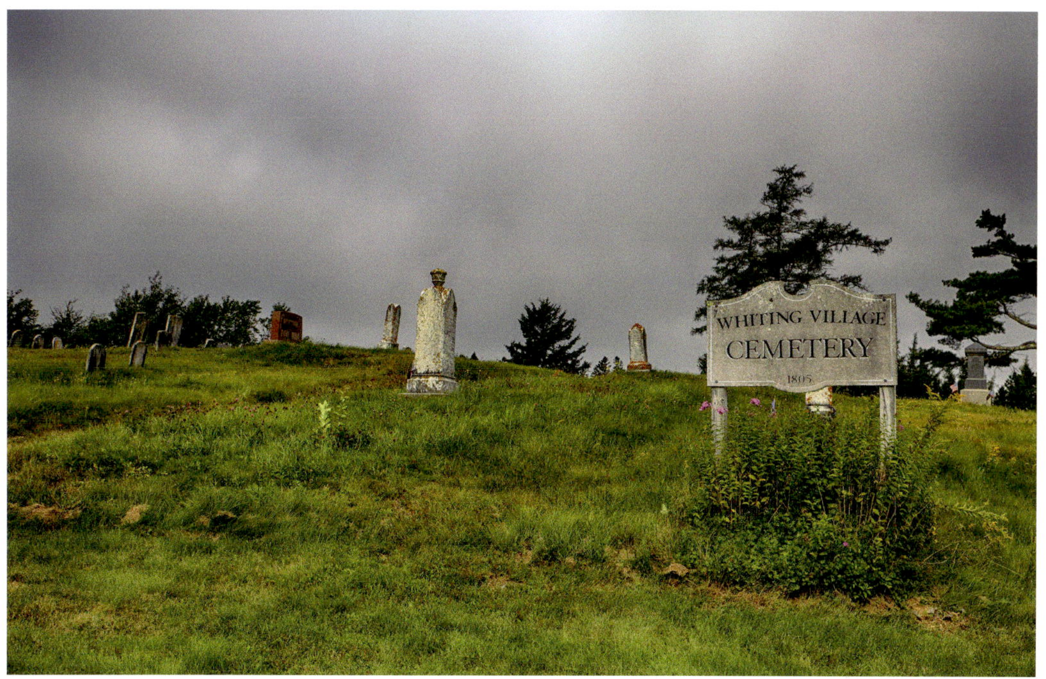

According to the 2020 census, the population in Whiting, Maine, was 482. Originally named Orangetown, it was renamed Whiting after early settler Tate Whiting.

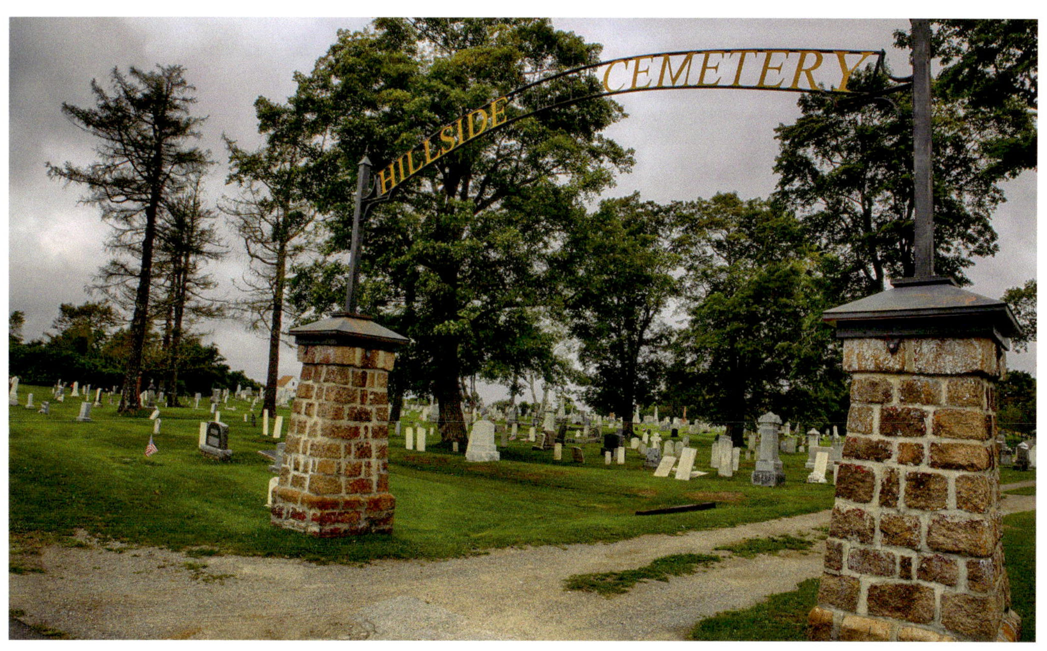

This cemetery is in Maine's easternmost city and is a perfect indicator of the area's rich history. Sea captains, British soldiers, American soldiers, Civil War heroes, and so much more can all be found here.

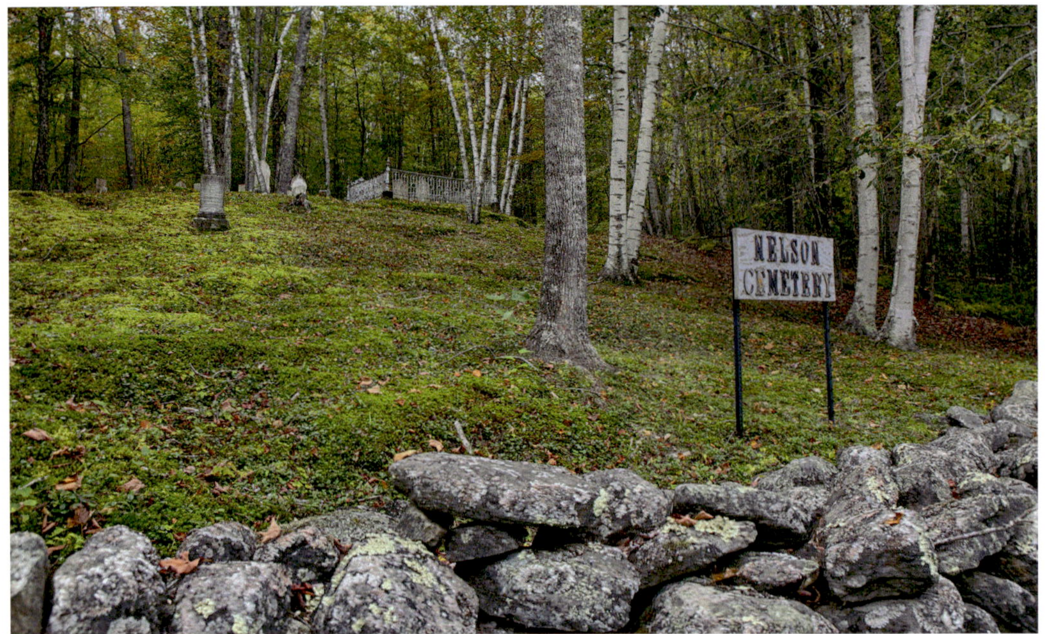

This small hillside cemetery in Knox County holds only thirty-two interments and is in a secluded wooded area. It was active throughout the nineteenth century, into the early 1900s.

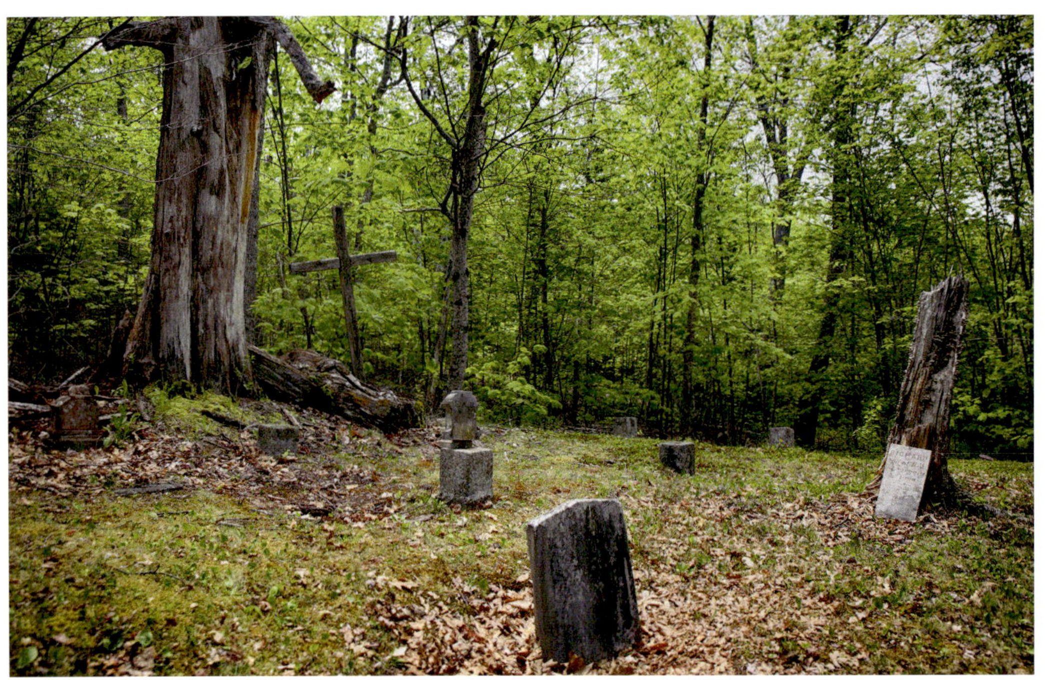

The old wooden cross in the back of this cemetery has a rotten base and it leans precariously to one side. This Penobscot County graveyard has the appearance of being very neglected.

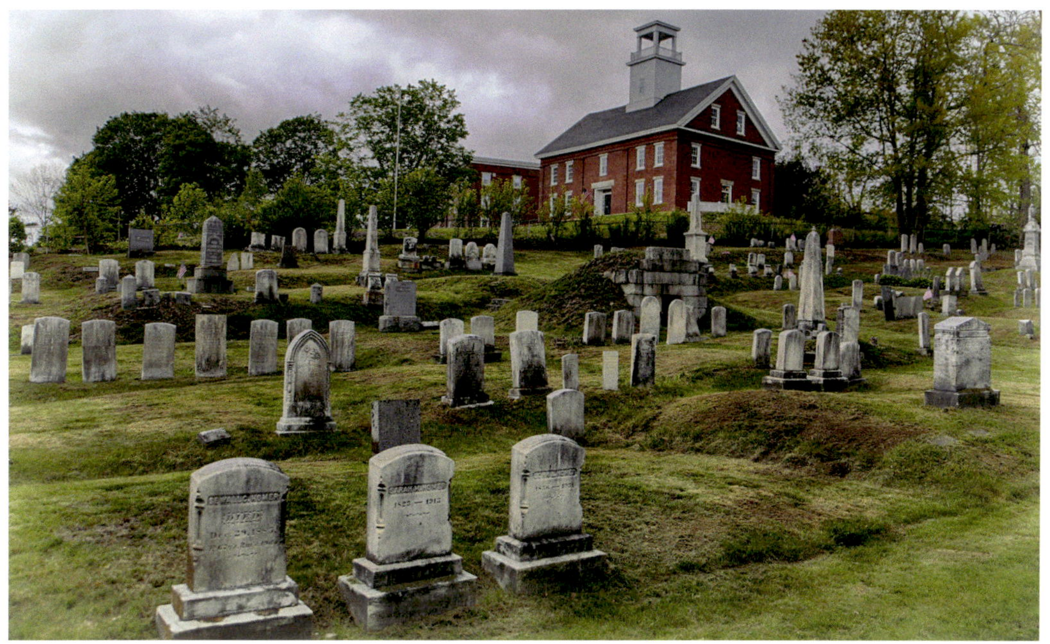

An abandoned seminary school looms in the background at Oak Hill Cemetery in Bucksport. Construction here led to the discovery of large deposits of the red clay once used by the Red Paint People.

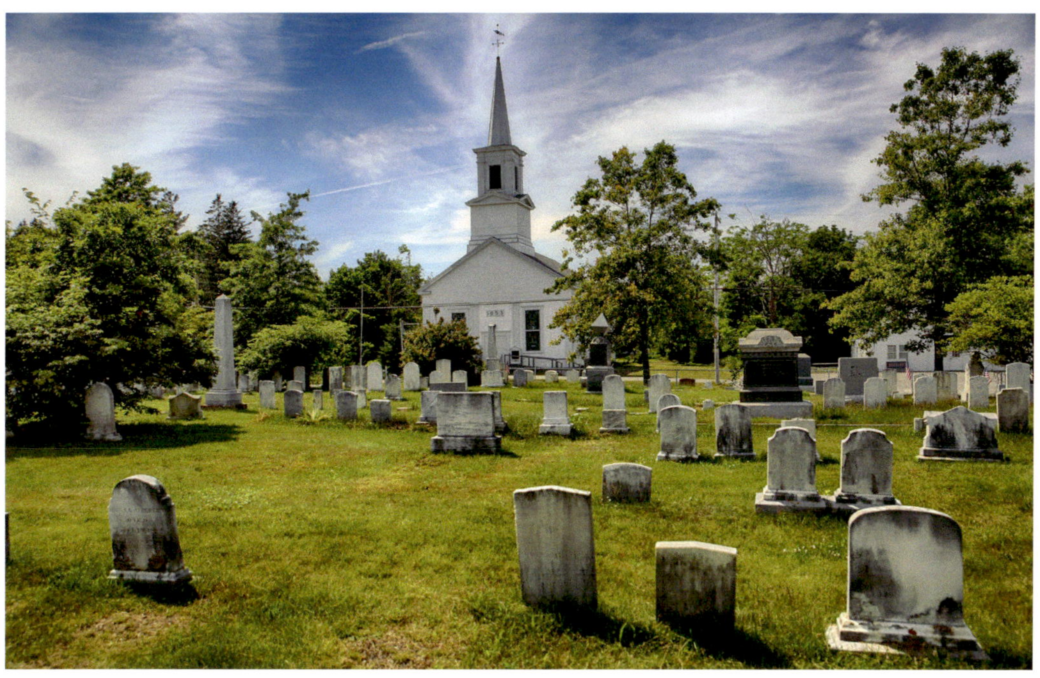

The Brooklin Cemetery looking out toward the Brooklin First Baptist Church. According to the 2020 U.S. census, the small village community in Hancock County has a population of around 827.

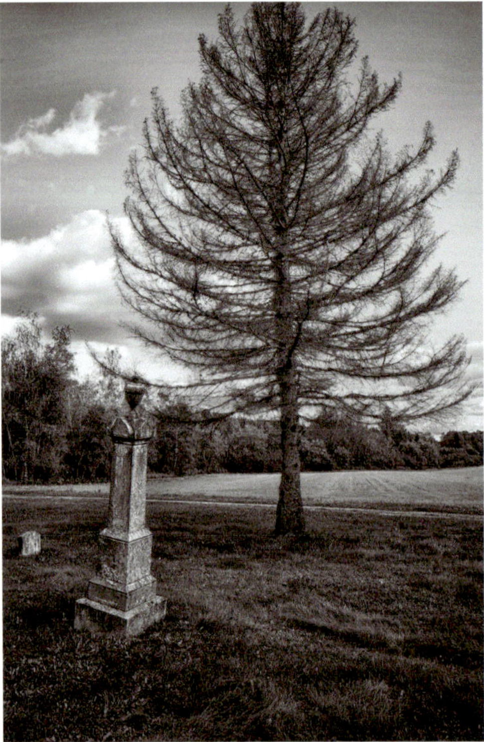

Somewhere in Aroostook County, a nineteenth-century monument stands starkly against a dead fir tree. In the background, an untilled potato field is the only thing near this old family graveyard.

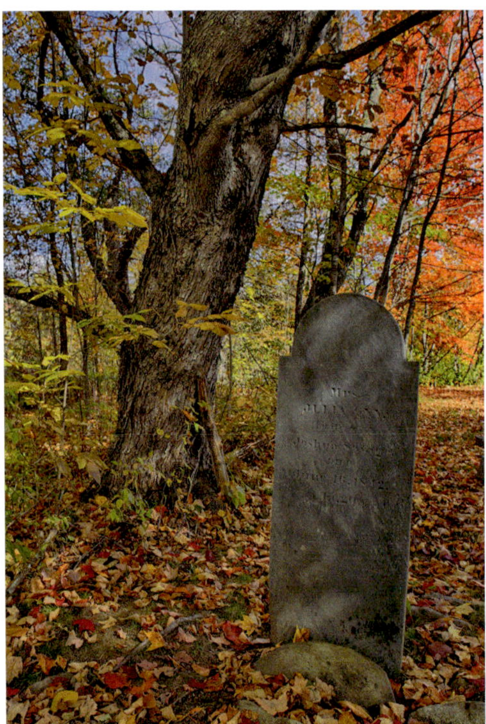

Julia Ann Savage rests under the shade of a large oak tree in the corner of a small family burial plot. She died at the age of twenty on June 16, 1842, and was survived by her husband, Joshua. Her epitaph reads, "She died in Jesus and was blest, How sweet her slumbers are from suffering, and from sin released and freed from every snare."

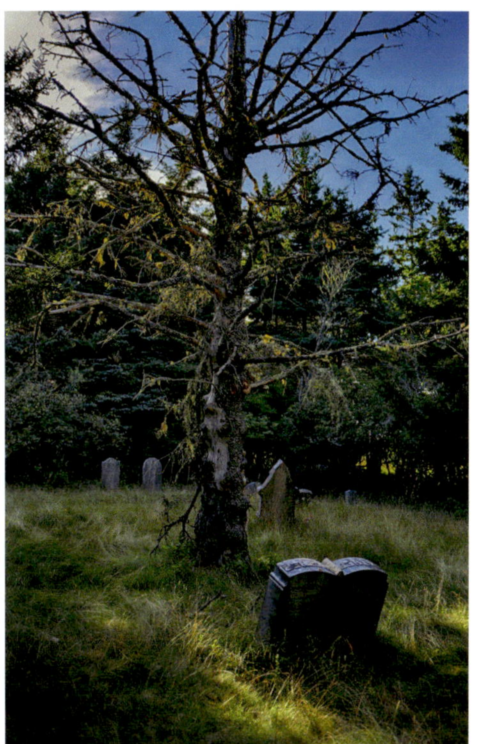

The evening sun setting in an overgrown cemetery, image used for the poem "Last Gleam."

Last Gleam

As the last gleam begins to fade,
evening sorrows beckon the night.
Shadows stir as the gloom takes hold
and silhouettes stalk in stillness,
swallowing slowly dying light

The flower's bloom withers and dies,
and only stark remnants prevail
In the dark, Death is welcome
as the day loses its grasp
to the Lord of Night

Conclusion

It is inevitable that we are all going, but where we are heading remains in question. Speaking through his character in the play *Hamlet*, Shakespeare referred to death as "The undiscovered country. From whose bourne no traveler returns."[1] As Shakespeare and countless others have alluded to, what is yet undiscovered cannot be known, only speculated upon as we journey to that final destination.

This book has not explored death in as much as it has explored the lives that came before those inevitable ends. Who knows where this journey's end will lead. It is not for us to know. However, we can have some control as we travel to that uncertain place, and it is up to us to live in such a way that we would wish to have reflected on our epitaphs.

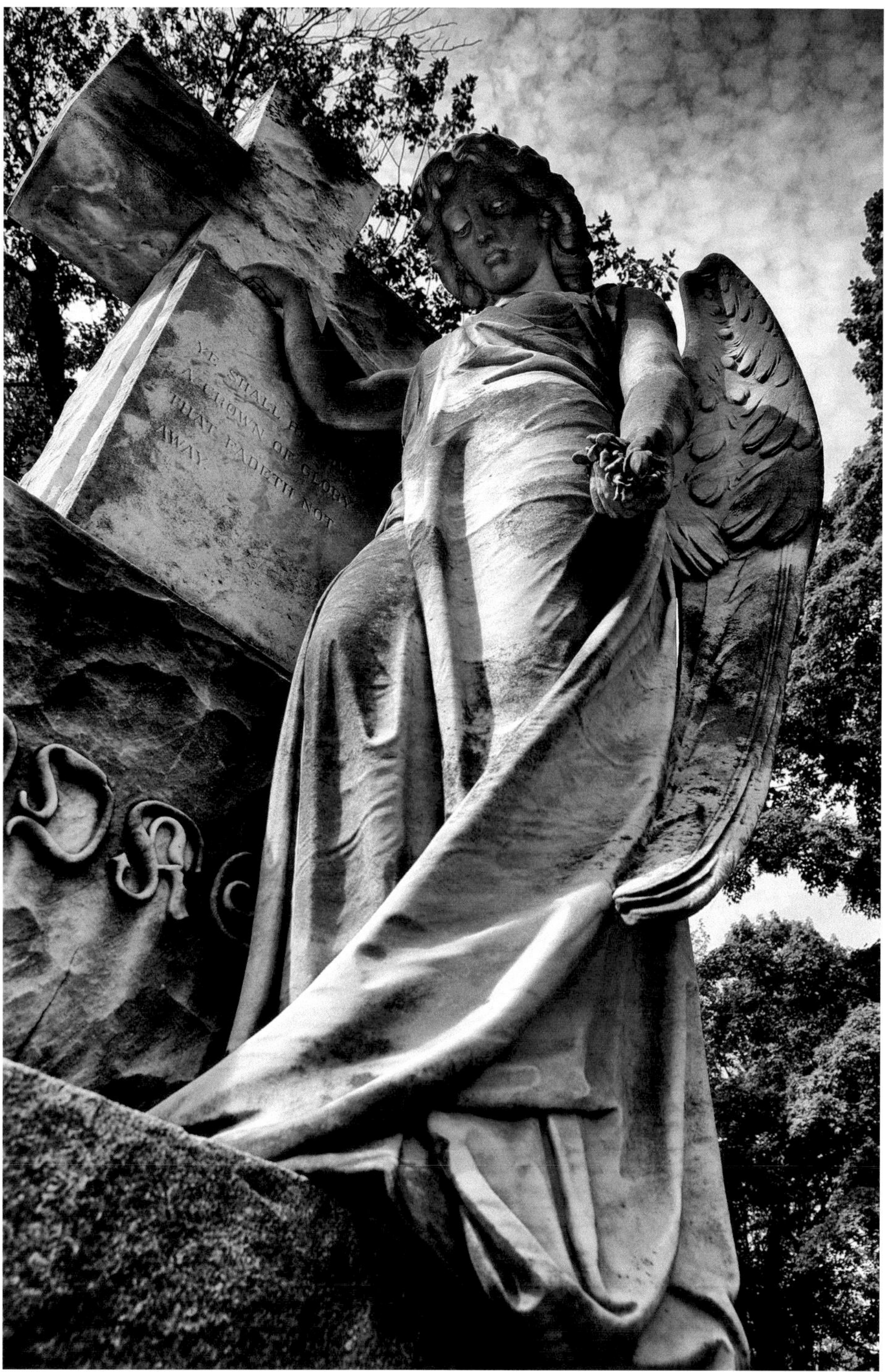

Angels exist in many mythologies and have many tasks; guiding souls along the path to salvation is perhaps their best-known task.

Endnotes

Epigraph

1 Wilde, O., "Requiescat," *Poems* (Boston, *Roberts Brothers*, 1881), pp. 37–38.

Preface

1 Poe, E. A., "*The Premature Burial,*" *Complete Tales & Poems of Edgar Allen Poe* (*Castle Books*, 2002), p. 217.

Introduction

1 Thomas, D., "*Do Not Go Gentle into That Good Night,*" *The Poems of Dylan Thomas* (*New Directions Publishing Corporation,* 1952), p. 207.

Chapter 1

1 Moorehead, W. K., "The Red-Paint People of Maine," *American Anthropologist*, vol. 15, no. 1, 1913, pp. 33–47. JSTOR, www.jstor.org/stable/659556. Accessed October 10, 2023.

Chapter 2

1 "The Old Burying Ground" sign. Maine Department of Agriculture, Conservation and Forestry, Division of Parks and Public Lands. Viewed May 28, 2023.

Chapter 3

1 McDermott, D., "Burying Yard 'Marks the Rise of York,'" Seacoastonline, July 5, 2016, www.seacoastonline.com/story/news/local/2016/07/05/burying-yard-marks-rise-york/27541089007/. Accessed October 10, 2023.

CHAPTER 5

1 Robinson, E. A., "For a Dead Lady," *The Town Down The River* (New York, Charles Scribner's Sons, 1910), pp. 114–115.
2 White, E. B., "XXI: Last Day," *Charlotte's Web* (Harper and Row, Publishers, 1952), p. 164.

CHAPTER 6

1 Burnham, E., "The Real Story of Bucksport Namesake Jonathan Buck Has Nothing to Do With a Witch's Curse," *Bangor Daily News*, July 16, 2019, www.bangordailynews.com/2019/07/16/news/the-real-story-of-bucksport-namesake-jonathan-buck-has-nothing-to-do-with-a-witchs-curse. Accessed October 10, 2023.
2 Whittemore, J. O., "The Witch's Curse: A Legend of an Old Maine Town," *New England Magazine*, vol. New Series, Vol. 27, September 1902–February 1903, p. 112.
3 Coffin, R. P. T., "The Foot of Tucksport," *Collected Poems of Robert P. Tristram Coffin* (The Macmillan Company, 1939), pp. 180–190.
4 "York in American History: The Witch's Grave, Myth and History," *The York Weekly*, Seacoastonline, October 27, 2020, www.seacoastonline.com/story/news/local/york-weekly/2020/10/27/york-american-history-witchs-grave-myth-and-history/3747956001, Accessed October 10, 2023.
5 Emery, G. A., "Spirits-Haunted House," *Ancient city of Gorgeana and modern town of York Maine from its earliest settlement to the present time* (Boston, G. A. Emery, 1873), pp. 127–130.
6 Lunt, W., "A Matter of Historical Folklore: Laughing and Playful Sister Spirits Haunt Chute Road Graveyard," *The Windham Eagle Lifestyles*, October 23, 2020, lifestyles.thewindhameagle.com/2020/10/a-matter-of-historical-folklore.html. Accessed October 13, 2023.

CHAPTER 7

1 "Brady Gang," FBI, May 18, 2016, www.fbi.gov/history/famous-cases/brady-gang. Accessed October 9, 2023.
2 Russell, J., "Bangor recalls Brady Gang," *The Boston Globe*, October 6, 2007.
3 Public Domain Image. Digital commons, Bangor Public Library, digicom.bpl.lib.me.us/spc_brady_img. Accessed May 5, 2023.
4 Public Domain Image. Digital commons, Bangor Public Library, digicom.bpl.lib.me.us/spc_brady_img. Accessed May 5, 2023.
5 Public Domain Image. Digital commons, Bangor Public Library, digicom.bpl.lib.me.us/spc_brady_img. Accessed May 5, 2023.
6 Public Domain Image. Digital commons, Bangor Public Library, digicom.bpl.lib.me.us/spc_brady_img. Accessed May 5, 2023.

CHAPTER 8

1 "America's Wars," Department of Veterans Affairs, www.va.gov/opa/publications/factsheets/fs_americas_wars.pdf. Accessed October 12, 2023.

CONCLUSION
1 Shakespeare, W., *Hamlet* (AmazonClassics, 2017), p. 91.

Further Reading

On Jonathan Buck

Goudsward, D., "Haverhill's Cursed Son: Jonathan Buck," WHAV—Greater Haverhill's Only Public Radio Station and Nonprofit Local News Service, October 23, 2016, whav. net/2016/10/23/haverhills-cursed-son-jonathan-buck/
Heath, O. M., *Composts of Tradition: Jonathan Buck, His Curse* (O.M. Heath and Co., 1913), pp. 121–57
Hempstead, B. D., M. A., Rev. A. G., "Legends of the Buck Monument," The 150th Anniversary of Bucksport, Maine, *The Bucksport Free Press*, June 1942, pp. 28–30
"The Witch's Curse Fulfilled," *The Republican Journal*, vol. 80, no. 49, December 1908, p. 3. Library of Congress, www.loc.gov/item/sn78000873/1908-12-03/ed-1/

On Joshua Chamberlain

Lange, K., "Army Maj. Gen. Joshua Chamberlain," U.S. Department of Defense, February 24, 2020, www.defense.gov/News/Feature-Stories/story/Article/2086560/medal-of-honor-monday-army-maj-gen-joshua-chamberlain

On Smith-Anderson Cemetery

Lunt, W., "Before the Memory Fades: The Hauntings on River Road," *The Windham Eagle Lifestyles*, November 4, 2022, lifestyles.thewindhameagle.com/2022/11/before-memory-fades-hauntings-on-river.html
Pal, H., "It Happened in Windham: Take a Walk through History," *Press Herald*, November 1, 2019, www.pressherald.com/2019/11/01/it-happened-in-windham-take-a-walk-through-history/
"Smith Anderson Cemetery—FrightFind," FrightFind, frightfind.com/smith-anderson-cemetery/. Accessed November 15, 2023

On York Witch

Owen, R. W., "The Town Farm—A Victorian-Era Solution to Poverty—Forgotten New England," *Forgotten New England*, October 12, 2011, forgottennewengland.com/2011/10/11/youre-going-to-send-us-to-the-poor-fahm/
"The 1692 Indian Massacre at York Maine," *Maine Genealogy*, December 11, 2020, mainegenealogy.com/york/the-1692-indian-massacre-at-york-maine.htm